HOW OPERATI[...] STRATEGY

Justin Kelly
Mike Brennan

September 2009

Visit our website for other free publication downloads
http://www.StrategicStudiesInstitute.army.mil/

To rate this publication click here.

*****

Comments pertaining to this report are invited and should be forwarded to: Director, Strategic Studies Institute, U.S. Army War College, 122 Forbes Ave, Carlisle, PA 17013-5244.

*****

All Strategic Studies Institute (SSI) publications are available on the SSI homepage for electronic dissemination. Hard copies of this report also may be ordered from our homepage. SSI's homepage address is: *www.StrategicStudiesInstitute.army.mil*.

*****

The Strategic Studies Institute publishes a monthly e-mail newsletter to update the national security community on the research of our analysts, recent and forthcoming publications, and upcoming conferences sponsored by the Institute. Each newsletter also provides a strategic commentary by one of our research analysts. If you are interested in receiving this newsletter, please subscribe on our homepage at *www.StrategicStudiesInstitute.army. mil/newsletter/*.

ISBN 1-58487-402-3

CONTENTS

FOREWORD

The publication of the 1982 version of Army Field Manual (FM) 100-5, *Operations*, introduced to the English-speaking world the idea of an operational level of war which encompassed the planning and conduct of campaigns and major operations. It was followed 3 years later by the introduction of the term "operational art" which was, in practice, the skillful management of the operational level of war. This conception of an identifiably separate level of war that defined the jurisdiction of the profession of arms was, for a number of historical and cultural reasons, attractive to U.S. practitioners and plausible to its English-speaking allies. As a result, it and its associated doctrine spread rapidly around the world.

This monograph argues that the idea of an operational level of war charged with the planning and conduct of campaigns misconceives the relationship between wars, campaigns, and operations, and is both historically mistaken and wrong in theory. Brigadier Justin Kelly (Australian Army Retired) and Dr. Michael Brennan conclude that its incorporation into U.S. doctrine has had the regrettable impact of separating the conduct of campaigns from the conduct of wars and consequently marginalized the role of politics in the direction of war. In essence, they argue that the idea of the campaign has come to overwhelm that of strategy.

This monograph argues that as warfare continues to diffuse across definitional and conceptual boundaries and as the close orchestration of all of the instruments of national power becomes even more important, the current conception of campaigns and operations becomes crippling. To cope with these demands by formulating and prosecuting "national campaigns," the authors propose that the responsibility for campaign design should "actually" return to the political-strategic leadership of nations supported by the entirety of the state bureaucracy. This would mark the return of the campaign to its historical sources. If the United States and its allies fail to make this change, they risk continuing to have a "way of battle" rather than a "way of war."

DOUGLAS C. LOVELACE, JR.
Director
Strategic Studies Institute

SUMMARY

There was a time when the world had no need for operational art, a time when sovereigns led their armies in the field and where the yoking of war to politics was their personal undertaking. It was the sovereign who chose whether or not to fight, where to fight, how long to fight, and it was they who were constantly balancing opportunities and threats, risks and returns, costs and benefits. In the era of "strategies of a single point," the connections between tactics and statecraft were immediate and intimate. As modern states emerged, their economic and social organization enabled them to deploy and sustain armies of ever increasing size. Big armies needed more space, and the theater of operations grew along with them. This increasingly removed the actions of those armies from the direct scrutiny of the sovereign, and the connection between war and politics became unacceptably stretched.

The idea of the campaign was expanded to redress this widening gap, and it gained a geographic meaning in addition to its traditional temporal one. The campaign became the pursuit of the war's objectives by an independent commander acting beyond the immediate scrutiny of his sovereign. The framework provided by the campaign objectives, geographic boundaries, resources, and other guidance provided by the sovereign determined the freedom of action available to the campaign commander. Within those freedoms, he was able to sequence battles as he thought necessary in order to achieve the objectives that had been provided to him. Most likely a number of tactical action sequences connected by a unifying idea, i.e., "operations," each directed at somehow setting the conditions for the next step, would be necessary. The cascading hierarchy of objectives—political, strategic, campaign, operational, and tactical—reconnected tactical action to the political purposes of the war.

These thoughts had emerged by the late-19th century and were further developed and adorned as the experience of total war grew through World Wars I and II. Although they had been a part of U.S. doctrine until after World War I, they disappeared for awhile, and it was not until the 1982 version of U.S. Army Field Manual (FM) 100-5 that these ideas were reintroduced, although in a different form. Rather than meeting its original purpose of contributing to the attainment of campaign objectives laid down by strategy, operational art—practiced as a "level of war"—assumed responsibility for campaign planning. This reduced political leadership to the role of "strategic sponsors," quite specifically widening the gap between politics and warfare. The result has been a well-demonstrated ability to win battles that have not always contributed to strategic success, producing "a way of battle rather than a way of war."

The political leadership of a country cannot simply set objectives for a war, provide the requisite materiel, then stand back and await victory. Nor should the nation or its military be seduced by this prospect. Politicians should be involved in the minute-to-minute conduct of war; as Clausewitz reminds us, political considerations are "influential in the planning of war, of the campaign, and often even of the battle." As war continues to diffuse across definitional and conceptual boundaries and as enemies seek ways to exploit democracy's vulnerabilities, closing the gap between politics and the conduct of war is becoming ever more important.

It is time we returned what we now call campaign design to the political and strategic leadership of the country and returned operational art to its original venue, where it was overwhelmingly concerned with tactics.

ALIEN:
HOW OPERATIONAL ART DEVOURED STRATEGY

PREFACE

> The purpose of such an innovation [operational art] is unclear ... in western military science operational art as a theoretical concept is completely rejected. . . . The West should not add this concept to its armory.

> Walter Jacobs
> *Army*, November 1961

In most fields of military endeavor, theory has had only a modest influence on praxis. Faced with real problems, the militaries of the world generally set about contriving practical solutions in a more or less theory-free environment, generating the seeds of new theory as a by-product. Theory, however, is influential in the preparation for war; bad theory risks leading us into poor preparations. Analyses of the consequences of poor preparation for war line the bookcases of most of the people reading this monograph.

In recent times many have theorized about the character of contemporary conflict, introducing relatively new ideas such as systems theory into our understanding while retaining much of our original lexicon. In this necessary process, occasionally the original context is lost or abandoned, sometimes resulting in confusion, error, and dilution of meaning. This monograph focuses on one key phrase of the soldier's lexicon—operational art. Operational art is a term whose original context has been lost, and its meaning has been consequently stretched beyond useful limits. The exercise of operational art has come to represent the pinnacle of the profession of arms and the core of its professional jurisdiction. Partially as a result of this, its relationship with campaign planning has been clouded, and it has come to compete with strategy rather than being its humble servant.

The militaries of the world had always used terms like "operation" and "operational" but they had multiple meanings and usages. It was only towards the end of the 19th century that a special meaning of operation—as a succession of tactical actions sharing a single unifying idea—was defined and began to pass generally into doctrine. After the catharsis of World War I, military theorists in the Union of Soviet Socialist Republics (USSR) began to write about "operational art," the skillful design and execution of operations, as a discrete and identifiable subject worthy of intensive theoretical examination.

Most of the debate surrounding the codification of operational art took place in languages other than English. As a result, the debate was largely invisible to the Anglophone world. This changed dramatically in 1982 with the publication of U.S. Army Field Manual (FM) 100-5, *Operations*, which reintroduced English speakers to the idea that the area between strategy and tactics might not be entirely vacant. For reasons that are unclear, the relatively neat Soviet idea of operational art became, via FM 100-5, the "operational level of war." We argue that this transition was a theoretical solecism creating complications for the application of operational art, and further that we may not be able to overcome these complications in the context of contemporary wars. Wrong-headed theory has been translated into doctrine and is now hindering rather than supporting the conduct of war.

As originally proposed by the Soviets, operational art was confined firmly within a context provided by a campaign plan arrived at by strategy and was constrained in its responsibilities to the attainment of discrete identifiable objectives within that campaign. In western usage it has come to encompass both that meaning plus *the design, planning, and conduct of campaigns*. One can reasonably argue that *"a rose by any other name is still a rose"* — that, for example, campaigns clearly need to be designed and that if we call this process "operational art" it does not matter that we are diverging from the classical usage of the term. But such an argument ignores the subsequent questions of who then designs and executes "operations" in the classical meaning of the word and what is the residual role for strategic leadership. Arguably, the concern occasionally aired about the "compression of the operational level of war" is a symptom of this theoretical confusion and actually demonstrates strategy reasserting its traditional and proper role in the face of a faddish usurper.

With emerging theoretical frameworks like *systemic operational design, effects-based operations*, the British *comprehensive approach*, and Australia's *adaptive campaigning*, we are attempting to take operational art into new and largely uncharted territory where theorists and practitioners alike will be asking it to deal with circumstances encompassing a degree of complexity that has not hitherto been its lot. Under these concepts we expect operational artists to align all the instruments of national power to help resolve a military problem. As developed here, in the not too distant past this was the purview of the national leader, executing national strategy from a position on, or near, the battlefield. If operational art is now associated with an independent level of war, personified in the presence of an independent operational commander charged with the design and execution of campaigns, then we are asking an individual at the periphery to organize the center from which the other instruments of national power receive their direction. This is confused at best. If readers accept that leadership of the center from the periphery is problematic, then "we" need to exercise peer leadership at the center to achieve the level of national and international coordination that is described in our doctrine. This is surely beyond the purview of operational art or of an operational commander. Campaign design and planning are correctly a product of strategy and must occur either in national capitals or at least within the national strategic leadership.

Recent western military exploits in Iraq, Somalia, Rwanda, Bosnia, Kosovo, Afghanistan, and East Timor, all represent, if not strategic failure, at least failures of strategy. The question we need to ask ourselves is whether this weakness is endemic or at least partially a result of our own theoretical failings by allowing operational art to escape from any reasonable delimitation and, by so doing, subvert the role of strategy and hide the need for a strategic art? Also to the point, how well does our existing theoretical framework enable us to adapt to the demands of contemporary conflict? This monograph attempts to answer such questions.

INTRODUCTION

> [T]he prime requirement of operational command
> is creativity [which] implies the cognitive powers
> to deal with the complexities of abstract strategic
> aims and the ability to assemble a series of tactical
> actions into an abstract outcome" — which in nearly
> all situations will be the submission of the enemy.
>
> Shimon Naveh[1]

Wars are fought to achieve a distribution of political power that is satisfactory to the victor. Political power rests on the acquiescence of a population, however that is attained. Therefore, the fundamental challenge in war is to assemble a sequence of actions that seems likely to change the minds of a hostile population. Some stratagems, tactics, or weapons may be, or become, inimical to that shift in the popular consensus and be counterproductive. Some may have mixed impacts — influencing different parts of the target community in different ways. Actions to overcome armed resistance may alienate sectors of the population, while failing to do so may be a path to defeat. Shifts in the circumstances on the ground, in the domestic politics of the belligerents, or in the wider international community may validate, invalidate, or alter the strategic objectives being sought, the campaign plan being pursued, or the tactics being employed. Although these complexities are not new, they are becoming increasingly salient in our contemporary setting.

The aphorism that "strategy proposes but tactics disposes" is valid. Unless strategy includes a tactical view, it may seek objectives which are practically unachievable, or it may miscalculate the costs and benefits likely to emerge from a conflict. These costs are

5

not limited to the direct economic and social impacts of war on the belligerents but extend to international public opinion and international politics. The consequences of tactical actions can, more than ever, now decide not just who wins the war but also the shape of the peace that follows it.[2] Equally, tactics needs to serve strategy, and tactical action without strategic purpose is merely senseless violence. The strategic direction of a war needs to be intimately sensitive to the details of the warfare being conducted so as to ensure both that it is making realistic demands, and that the military action remains in keeping with the wider conduct of the war. Moreover, tactics needs to be constantly seeking to contribute to the ends laid down by strategy with economy, efficiency, and nuance, the latter being shaped by an awareness of the wider conduct of the war. A two-way conversation between strategy and tactics is fundamental to the successful prosecution of any war.

Sound theory attempts to deal with this reality. The German school of military theorists that emerged around the end of the 18th century, for example, saw war as a "giant demonic force, a huge spiritual entity, surcharged with brutal energy."[3] For those responsible for the management of this beast, it was clear that to be understood and properly directed war needed to be seen in the round. As Herbert Scharnhorst usefully reminded us, "One must habitually consider the whole of war before its components."[4] Michael Handel expands on this proposition, arguing that war needs to be viewed as a *Gestalt*, or complex whole comprising concrete and abstract elements: "[B]ecause of its infinite complexity and non-linear nature, war can only be understood as an organic whole, not as a mere compendium of various separate elements."[5]

Today systems theory reinforces this understanding, reminding us that war should be seen as one cluster of emergent behaviors of an enormously complex system and as one that will develop its own emergent behaviors according to its initial conditions and infinitely small changes in its environment, truly "more than a chameleon." Systems theory also informs us that attempts to establish absolute control over such a complex adaptive system are futile, and the best that can be hoped for is to damp undesirable behaviors and reinforce desirable ones to sustain the system in an equilibrium that, if not ideal, is at least recognizable.

In a recent article in *Military Review*, Huba Wass de Czega described the difficulty of attempting to realize some idealized condition within the dynamism of real wars. He compares the existing doctrinal approach of setting an objective and "going for it," with "the foundational discourses of the Confucian and Taoist east [which] do not frame life experience in terms of idealized ends or 'visions'." Chinese sages thought it impossible to know what an idealized end could be. They did not trust the mind to have a mirror-like correspondence to external reality. Instead they thought that distinguishing "better" from "worse" was the best one could do. Life experience, in their eastern perspective, was a perpetual and ever changing flow of events. Intellectual energy, in flowing with the way of the world, should ideally focus on understanding the forces, tendencies, and propensities of the contextual situation. In their understanding, one harmonizes with existence by enhancing the forces tending to flow toward "better," while subtly diverting and blocking those tending toward "worse."[6]

To cope with this fundamental dynamism and at the risk of oversimplification, the art of war can be characterized as a continuous conversation between strategic **ends**, i.e., that which is to be achieved; and tactical **means**, i.e., that which is to be done. Strategic propositions are invariably abstract, and tactical actions are necessarily concrete. The array of feasible tactical actions can be combined in any number of **ways** to create conditions that appear to be conducive to the original strategic proposition. The management of this conversation among ends, ways, and means is the art of war. It is an art because there is nothing fixed in the connections between them. The results of tactical action might not have the strategic consequences that were being sought; because the conversation is not conducted in isolation and the enemy gets a vote, forced changes may occur.[7] Therefore, as a war progresses, the strategic ends of the belligerents will usually evolve steadily. In the constant search for fleeting asymmetrical advantage, the tactical means chosen will undergo continuous and sometimes radical change. If the ends and the means change, the ways necessarily will need to change as well.

This dynamism has two consequences for theory. First, war needs to be managed as a whole — with the two-way conversation between strategy and tactics also being a continuous one. Second, any attempts to gain understanding by breaking a system into its constituent parts, in this case strategy-operations-tactics, isolate in theory what are united in praxis. As a result, such analysis generates theory that is practically and literally meaningless. The English-speaking world has grown to have a linear view of war, with ends, ways, and means arranged hierarchically and linked to discrete levels of command. At least implicitly, most of the conversation is one-way traffic: strategy directs and tactics obeys. This is war on Henry Ford's assembly line with Frederick Taylor measuring progress. It demeans the importance of the continuous and intimate two-way conversation that is essential for success. A more satisfactory perspective would notice that these are nested. These two contending views are shown diagrammatically at Figure 1. In practice—but not in our current theory—tactics and operational art are a part of—and not subordinate to—strategy.

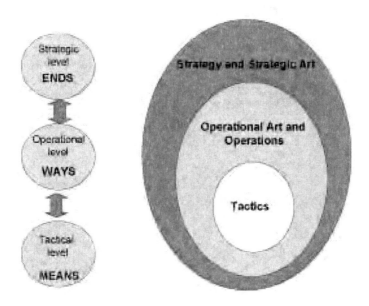

Figure 1. Two Contending Views of the Ends-Ways-Means Relationship.

This is more than a semantic difference. By taking a hierarchical view and linking discrete responsibilities to specific levels of command, we risk degrading the intimacy of the conversation among ends, ways, and means, making it easier for strategy to make unreasonable demands; for example, in Iraq in 2003-

06, with ways overtaking ends; or in 1950, MacArthur's precipitate pursuit to the Yalu, with tactics to taking on a life of its own. The reason the strategic corporal is strategic is that his world—tactics—is, and always has been, organic to strategy. This idea of the unity of war is especially important as we try to understand operational art. If we want to drag it into the sunlight to examine it in detail, we necessarily have to drag its strategic and tactical contexts with it.

We shall attempt to trace the evolution of operational art from its inception in the industrial revolution to its present form. We begin by examining Prussian practice in the mid-19th century and tracking the emergence and application of operational theory into and through the shared European experiences of World War I. After that war, the need to identify theoretical responses to the challenges it presented stimulated an explosion of new thinking in Germany, Russia, and Great Britain. The resultant differing responses to a shared problem are compared and contrasted. The emergence of operational art in the Anglophone world, specifically with the release of FM 100-5 in 1982, is then examined. Rather than simply translating existing theory and applying it in a new context, FM 100-5 created, we shall argue, a new and wrong theory, confusing operational art with strategy. We conclude with an examination of the impact of this confusion, the so-called Leavenworth Heresy, on approaches to contemporary conflict.

Our aim in this monograph is to explain what operational art originally meant and why it is time we returned this beast it to its enclosure.

THE TIME BEFORE

> As a rule, destroying the enemy's forces tends to be
> a gradual process.
>
> Clausewitz

The need for "operations" was a product of changes brought about by the the Napoleonic concept of the nation in arms and the impact of the industrial revolution. The nation in arms provided huge armies, while the Industrial Revolution provided the means to equip, deploy, command, and sustain them. Whereas in the wars of the 18th century armies in the field seldom exceeded 150,000 troops, Napoleon invaded Russia in 1812 with 600,000 men, while the Prussians invaded France in 1870 with 1,200,000. As a result of such increases, the size of the battlefield grew from a few kilometers wide in Frederick's time to several hundred kilometers in France in 1871.

The use of seemingly inexhaustible mass armies supported by the full economic power of increasingly well-organized states escalated warfare, at least in Europe, from limited wars of dynastic maneuvering to unlimited and stupendously violent wars seeking the complete subjugation of the enemy. This raised the stakes of war for the belligerents at the same time that the increased scope and dispersion of action reduced the ability to maintain tight control. Therefore, whereas it remained a common practice for European monarchs to accompany their armies into the field until well into the 19th century, the sovereign's presence no longer ensured that the means committed to tactical engagements remained yoked to strategic objectives.[8]

As a result of these influences, the conversation

between politics, strategy, and tactical action achieved a new importance for soldiers, as increasingly they would be the ones trying to make these connections. The need to examine this experience was the animating impulse for Carl von Clausewitz and Henri Jomini, who became the progenitors of the larger part of modern military theory. Despite some differences, both of these theorists considered the task of connecting battles as "strategy," to be used in the context of deciding where and when to fight to realize the purposes of a war.

There is a tendency for us today to try to herd Clausewitz and Jomini out of their corral and into our own. In this vein, it is not uncommon for those today to think that their failure to recognize the role of "operations" was simply the result of the absence of an appropriate term. To mend this "deficiency," we substitute "operations" for their use of "strategy." To do so is wrong. The reason these two great theorists did not suggest the existence of an intervening layer between strategy and tactics is that in their (Napoleonic) context, the need for such a layer did not exist. Kings and emperors, along with some trusted advisers, still customarily went to war and directed its conduct in pursuit of an acceptable outcome. Strategy directed tactics with great immediacy and intimacy. The decision as to whether to fight or not, where to fight, how to fight, and how long to fight, as well as what risks were acceptable and what costs bearable, were made "on the spot" by the head of state. There was no need or role for operations or operational art, and so neither Clausewitz nor Jomini proposed such a construct.

It has been suggested that Jomini introduced the term "Grand Tactics" to encapsulate what we now call operations. However, a careful reading indicates that grand tactics — "the art of posting troops upon the battlefield according to the characteristics of the ground" — was tactics pure and simple.[9] To strengthen this understanding, Jomini contrasts the "tactical combinations" of grand tactics with the more potent "strategic combinations" that threaten to make a general the "master of his enemy's communications while at the same time holding his own."[10] He thus describes strategy as the **"art of making war on the map [which] comprehends the whole theatre of operations,"**[11] whereas statesmanship decides "whether a war is proper, opportune, or indispensable and determines the various operations necessary to attain the object of the war,"[12] and military policy deals with "the political considerations relating to the operations of armies."[13] Jomini's view is thus complete and remains reasonable even today, describing, as it does, the sweep from operations and tactics to military strategy through national strategy. However, despite the creation of the bridging idea of "grand tactics," the extent of the overlap between each of the areas he defines prevents him from clearly articulating the connections between them. As a result, he ends up describing what a thing is but not how it works, and his utility to us is thus correspondingly modest.

In contrast, Clausewitz held a clear view that war was a *Gestalt* that could be understood only in terms of its political direction.[14] He described war as an extension of politics that were themselves the product of the interplay of rational, nonrational, and irrational influences mutually interacting in "the remarkable trinity." Therefore, political direction was not equated to rational policy but to rational policy shaped, circumscribed, and subverted by the irrational and nonrational forces inherent in the base polity.[15] At the same time, the realities of combat — chance, uncertainty, and friction — and the independent will of the enemy made warfare as dynamic and unpredictable as its political direction. Clausewitz understood the dynamism of war — why it was "more than a true chameleon" which only changes its skin color. In today's terminology, Clausewitz saw war as a complex system constantly threatening to escape human control, to lose coherence and slide into chaos. This recognition led him to postulate a theory of war based on how war might be prevented from losing its coherence, and he posited a systems view in which it was made coherent only by its political aim. To Clausewitz, keeping actions aligned behind the political aim was both the greatest challenge in warfare and the essence of good practice.

Clausewitz therefore argued that in war every action needed to contribute to the attainment of the political aim: "tactics teaches the use of the armed forces in the engagement. Strategy, the use of engagements for the object of the war."[16] Clausewitz's elegant explanation avoids the reductionism of Jomini, while providing incisive clarity as to the need to connect tactics (engagements or battles) directly to the attainment of the political objective of the war. As usual, Clausewitz is able to explain to us not just what something is, but how it works in practice.

Although Clauswitz separates the two ideas of "strategy" and "tactics" for didactic clarity, there is a strong caveat against considering them in isolation. Strategy proposes, but tactics disposes, or, in Clausewitz's terms, "all strategic planning rests on tactical success alone." As a result, although it is tempting to conduct discrete analyses of strategy and tactics, to do so is wrong. The ideas of strategy and tactics are fused, as are the ideas of "strategy" and "political aim." The dynamism of each influence on a war, from politics to minor tactics, together with the infinitely changeable connections between each them, means that war cannot be analyzed by dissection—it can only be understood as a complex and dynamic whole. War does not lend itself to analysis by levels.

Despite his clarity and utility, Clausewitz would probably be unknown to the English speaking world today had it not been for Helmuth von Moltke. The Austro-Prussian (1866) and the Franco-Prussian (1870-71) wars both concluded with the complete overthrow of seemingly more powerful enemies by the Prussians. With some justification, the responsibility for this success was ascribed to the military acumen of Prussian Chief of the General Staff von Moltke. As a result, his views on the nature and conduct of war, which he acknowledged rested heavily on his reading of Clausewitz, became of interest to the broad military community. Clausewitz thus came to the attention of the Anglophone world.[17]

The 1866 war was decided at the Battle of Königgrätz. In the approach to this battle, Moltke "flouted traditional theories about the advantages of operations on interior lines and demonstrated the manner in which space and movement could be used to encircle and destroy an army guided by conventional operational views."[18] Specifically, Königgrätz showed that "in an age in which industrial progress was making it possible to arm and transport armies which dwarfed those of antiquity, wars would be won by those nations which could raise, train, deploy, and command large armies most effectively" and that "wars of the future were going to be won . . . by operational plans which took account of such things as time, space, the increased size of modern armies, the available means of transportation, and the increased effectiveness of modern weaponry." In a particular situation, Moltke had given an impressive demonstration of how these factors must be related in an operational plan, dividing his army to assure the greatest possible speed in deployment, and "concentrating it not before, but during the battle, when concentration would have maximum effect."[19]

A number of aspects of the war of 1866 provided exemplars that would shape one arguably false view of operational art into the 21st century.[20] The mobilization and deployment of mass armies demanded time, space, and enormously detailed staff work. The process of calling-out corps and divisions, concentrating and victualling them, and directing them to the chosen theater of operations consumed time and road and rail space, all of which were in critically short supply. Moving the entire army as a concentrated mass would have created an unbearable burden on the road and rail infrastructure of 1860s Europe. Prussian staff organization—which was to become the exemplar for the rest of the world—dealt with these connected challenges by linking the call-out of troops with the availability of road and rail space to enable a dispersed approach march to the area in which the enemy was to be brought to battle. In essence, this meant that the means available for the decisive battle was directly and quite rigidly connected with the processes of national mobilization.

Moltke's plans in 1866 therefore dealt with connecting strategic decisions with a decisive battle through a bureaucratized process of mobilization and movement to set the stage for tactical action—what was called in German the "*Aufsmarsch*." This is not operational art. The War of 1866 was an old-fashioned war in which the campaign and the decisive battle essentially formed a singularity. The design of the campaign was overwhelmingly strategic, set out to create both the opportunity for a single decisive battle and the concentration of sufficient troops to provide a reasonable prospect of victory. In this context, the art of designing campaigns that align the instruments of national power to achieve strategic objectives clearly lies within the purview of strategy.

The War of 1866 did not exemplify operational art because there was no need for it. The Prussian King, Chancellor, and Chief of the General Staff deployed as a single Headquarters, providing robust connections between strategic objectives and the specific tactical actions taken. Although the Prussian army began its movement from dispersed locations, it aimed towards a single point which facilitated this intimate relationship. The birth of operational art itelf would need to await the events of 1870.[21]

THE EXPANSION OF WAR AND THE BIRTH OF OPERATIONAL ART

Although they are closely connected in time and necessarily share a number of similarities, between the wars of 1866 and 1870 there occurred a watershed in the evolution of operational art. Isserson describes a typical Napoleonic campaign as "a great, long approach, which engendered a long operational line, and a short final engagement in a single area, which, with respect to the long operational line is a single point in space and a single moment in time."[20] This echoes Clausewitz' interpretation of Napoleonic warfare: "The field of battle in the face of strategy is no more than a point; in precisely the same way the duration of battle reduces to a single moment in time." As a result, Isserson describes Napoleonic war as the era of single point strategy since "the entire mission of a military leader was reduced to concentrating all his forces at one point and throwing them into battle as a one act tactical phenomenon."[22]

In this sense, the war of 1866 demonstrated the strategy of a single point—Königgrätz—but, by 1870, the larger armies and more expansive theater of operations meant that this was no longer appropriate. In 1870-71 there were many battles that influenced each other and which extended through time and across space. War had outgrown the strategy of a single point. Whereas in 1866 all the Prussian armies moved towards Königgrätz, in 1870 the Germans' frontage was 100 km in their assembly areas, immediately increasing to 150 km as the force advanced. The defeat of France required four discrete combat links: Spichern-Werth, Metz, Sedan, and Paris, each of which represented a cluster of lesser battles of varying scale. This meant that battle, instead of occurring in a single place with the mass of the forces of both sides engaged, became distributed into a number of subordinate battles across a sometimes expanding front.[23] As a result, "Moltke was faced with a completely new problem of coordinating and directing combat efforts, tactically dissociated and dispersed in space to achieve the overall aim of defeating the enemy."[24]

As a consequence of this realization, towards the end of the 19th century German military thinkers were aware "that the battlefield had grown larger and deadlier." Battles and engagements had lost their distinctiveness and would blend into an all-encompassing "*Gesamtschlacht*" [overall battle] that might extend across the entire width and depth of the theater of war.[25] Of course, without some unification, the *Gesamtschlacht* would threaten to dissolve into an uncoordinated brawl. A framework to direct it was required. By 1895 at the latest, one had emerged, here described by Baron Colmar Von der Goltz:

> In the course of military events there will always be separate groups of affairs springing into prominence, the parts of which are more intimately connected with each other than the preceding or subsequent occurrences. Military activity then tends with livelier interest towards a special object and leaves all others to one side, or subordinates them, until the former is attained. After that, a certain abatement, or perhaps a brief pause for recuperation, may be observed until a more rapid course of action is again adopted, and, in a manner, a new idea, a second objective, becomes visible.
>
> Every such group of actions will be composed of marches, the assumption of positions, and combats, and is called an "operation." . . . That the different groups of occurrences . . . must be connected by the bond of a common leading thought, and not arbitrarily or accidentally strung together, is a matter of course, and does not remove the distinction.
>
> Again, among certain operations a more intimate relationship will generally be brought about by the fact that they are conducted under similar circumstance, at the same time of year, against the same hostile army and are separated from the rest of the operations through conditions of time or space, change of opponents or alteration in the method of conducting the war. Such an association of operations is called a "campaign," which forms a definite portion of the war.[26]

Therefore, at least in Germany by the end of the 19th century, there was an understanding that the evolution of warfare; the increasing size of armies; and improvements in firepower, communications, logistics, and the consequent expansion of theaters of operations, had created new conditions. These new conditions had led to the need to group tactical actions into "operations" and to group "operations" into "campaigns." As a result, strategy was faced with problems of a complexity new to it. Rather than war planning involving the design of a single campaign focused on creating the opportunity for a single decisive battle, it now possibly involved a need to plan several campaigns, each of which was itself a cluster of discrete and largely foreseen operations intended to achieve intermediate objectives combining to form the objective of the campaign as a whole. The summation of the objectives of each of the campaigns, in turn, represented the objectives of the war.

Between 1871 and World War I, war continued to expand as enlarged logistics capabilities increased the ability to assemble, distribute, and sustain masses of troops. In Europe in particular, strategic circumstances created imperatives to link the decision for war, national mobilization, and the national economy directly with the conduct of war. As a result, campaign plans were connected very directly with the highest strategic decisions and were a product of strategic planning which laid down a scheme of maneuver and allocated resources, objectives, timings, and axes of advance to each of them.

At the same time, the need to coordinate multiple blows distributed across time and space but supporting a single unifying idea broadened the understanding of the campaign (adding a geographic meaning to its previous temporal one) and created the special meaning of "operation" that we retain today. Within the campaign, clusters of tactical actions grouped in time or location and pursuing their own unifying idea—but one subordinate to that of the campaign— formed individual operations. The arrangement of these tactical actions and the retention of their focus on the campaign intent formed the entirety of the new, and as yet nameless, kid on the block—operational art. Whereas in 1866, the congruence of the war, the campaign, and the Battle of Königgrätz made operational art unnecessary, by 1870-71 it had become essential. It took until the end of the 19th century for this experience to be translated into theory and the test of World War I to prompt the initial theories to be revised and matured.

Annihilation.

> Victory through battle is the most important moment in war. Victory alone will break the will of the enemy and will subordinate his will to ours. Neither the capture of terrain, fortress, nor severance of lines of communication will achieve this objective. To achieve decision, breaking the will of the enemy through the destruction of his forces, that is the operational objective. This operational aim will then serve the needs of strategy. [27]

Moltke

Since he is commonly seen as one of the principal authors of modern operational art, it is important to note here the narrowness of one aspect of Moltke's conception. To him, the sole purpose of military action was to overthrow the enemy's means of resistance, that is, to destroy the enemy's army. Once disarmed, the enemy was by definition helpless, and the victor could dictate the terms for the subsequent peace. In this understanding, Moltke stood in line of succession connecting Napoleon with Clausewitz and Jomini, and through them with Alfred Graf von Schlieffen and 20th-century German and Russian theory. This idea of annihilation (in German *Vernichtungsgedanke*) and how it might be best achieved provide the thread unifying the subsequent development of Continental military thought. The cognitive processes of identifying where, when, and how the annihilating battles might be triggered, together with the management of risk in the context of time and space, of the belligerents' intentions and logistic capacities, and of the theater's logistical parameters, formed the basis of the art. Still, the underlying idea remained remarkably simple: to find, fix, and destroy the enemy army in the largest and most decisive battle that could be assembled.

Moltke saw that strategy bridged the gap from politics to tactics, i.e., that politics could not "be separated from strategy, for politics uses war to attain its objectives and has a decisive influence on a war's beginning and end. Politics does this in such a manner that it reserves to itself the right to increase its demands during the course of the war or to satisfy itself with minor successes."[28] He also saw that strategy dealt with establishing the setting for successful tactical action: "The first task of strategy is . . . the first deployment of the army. Here multifarious political, geographic, and national considerations come into question. . . . But these arrangements . . . must unfailingly lead to the intended result," which was "afford[ing] tactics the means for fighting and the probability of winning by the direction of armies and their meeting at the place of combat,"[29] with "the objective [being] . . . the hostile army insofar as it defends the object of the war."[30]

This last stipulation—"insofar as it defends the object of the war"—requires a little enlargement. Clausewitz enumerated the three main goals of every war:[31]

1. "To defeat the enemy armed force and destroy it. That means to direct the main effort first and always against the opponent's main army;

2. To take possession of the enemy's nonmilitary resources, i.e., occupation of the country or at least [take] action against the capital and other important strong points [at least partially because the enemy army was most likely to be found in front of such important assets]; and,

3. To win over public opinion [that is, to convince the population of the enemy state that they were defeated]. This goal may be achieved by great victories or possession of the capital."[32]

Despite this positive articulation in *On War*, he acknowledges that "the aim of disarming the enemy . . . is in fact not always encountered in reality, and need not be achieved as a condition of peace. On no account should theory raise it to the level of a law [for] . . . a variety of means are available to subdue the opponent's will."[33] Clausewitz links this caution to the idea of the means and ends of a particular war. If the ends are effectively unlimited, the total subjugation of a country for example, then the enemy's willpower will need to be totally disarmed, and this is likely to require that the three steps above be completed. In more limited wars, for example, where the object is to seize a province as a basis for negotiation, such an absolutist approach would be inappropriate.

In both the 1866 and 1870-71 wars, the object was the subjugation of the enemy state, and hence Moltke closely followed the Clausewitzian prescription. He moved on the enemy's capital (in 1866) and the enemy's fortresses (in 1871), thereby drawing the enemy armies into large battles which were won by Prussian tactical superiority (marginal in 1866 and marked in 1871), thereby placing the enemy capital at his mercy. Moltke, therefore, was pursuing a battle of annihilation (*Vernichtungschlacht*) because one was called for by theory.

Walter Goerlitz recounts a fascinating dialogue between Moltke and Frederick William, the Crown prince of Prussia, which highlights Moltke's focus on the French Army in the 1870 war:

> The Crown prince asked what would happen after Paris had been taken?
>
> Moltke: Then we shall push forward into the south of France in order to finally break the enemy's power.
>
> Crown Prince: But what will happen when our own strength is exhausted — when we can no longer win battles?
>
> Moltke. We must always win battles. We must throw France completely to the ground.
>
> Crown Prince: And what then?
>
> Moltke: Then we can dictate the kind of peace we want.
>
> Crown Prince: And if we ourselves bleed to death in the process?
>
> Moltke: We shall not bleed to death and, if we do, we shall have got peace in return.
>
> The Crown Prince then asked whether Moltke was informed about the current political situation, which might perhaps make such a course seem unwise. Moltke replied: "No, I have only to concern myself with military matters."[34]

In Moltke's mind, therefore, the design of a war, and its subordinate campaigns, was focused principally and overwhelmingly on the destruction of the enemy's army. Although, in 1870-71, he was seeking to destroy the French powers of resistance so as to enable the Prussians to dictate the kind of peace they wanted, he saw that his role was limited to setting the conditions for successful battle. Of course, in 1870-71, Moltke's headquarters was also the royal headquarters— which he shared with both his king and the Prussian Chancellor, Otto von Bismarck—both of whom acted vigorously and continuously to keep the conduct of the war aligned with its evolving political objectives.

As the battlefield expanded and the ability of strategy to exercise sufficient control to reliably assemble the instruments of "the" decisive battle declined, the role of operational art arose, though this entity was not yet christened with a formal name. Subordinate to a campaign aimed at annihilating the enemy, operational art was itself focused on its contribution to annihilation through the creation of opportunities for tactical battle under advantageous conditions. Because of this tactical focus, operational art evolved to create conditions for tactical actions that promised to impose the greatest possible attrition on the enemy. With the exception of the British School (of which more later), this focus on wholesale attrition unifies the subsequent evolution of operational theory.

OPERATIONAL ART IN GERMANY

The Bureaucratization of War.

In the lead-up to World War I, then, there was recognition that there was need to yoke geographically and temporally separate combat efforts to some unified scheme of maneuver, that battles remained the only decisive instrument in warfare, and that a succession of blows was necessary to defeat mass armies fielded by modern states.[35]

At the same time, by 1905 armies 20 times the size of those that had fought in 1870 confronted each other in central Europe. Each minute a brigade of 3,000 men with its artillery could discharge a volume of fire equal to that of the whole of Wellington's army of 60,000 soldiers firing volley and salvo at Waterloo.[36] Schlieffen, Chief of the German General Staff from 1891, noted that the problem was not how to kill with these deadly instruments, but how to defend against them.[37] It is difficult from the perspective of the 21st century to fully imagine how it was that armies of such a size, with their hunger for supplies of all sorts, could be maneuvered and sustained, given the transport infrastructure of central Europe in the late-19th century. Roads remained largely unsealed and designed to meet only the needs of the local economy, while railroads, although expanding rapidly, were still of limited capacity, unevenly distributed, and, at least initially, aimed at meeting economic needs rather than military ones. Other than rail locomotives, motive power was provided by draught animals or human toilers. In this infrastructural context, Central European powers needed to deploy armies of four to six million men, plus possibly more than a million horses, and then maneuver and sustain them in battle.

As a result, the importance of railroads for the deployment, maneuver, and support of armies, which had begun to emerge as a factor in 1870, came to dominate military planning in the lead-up to World War I since any network decisions taken in one place necessarily impacted on the remainder. If a network is working at its maximum capacity, its flexibility is necessarily constrained. As a result, the reliance by the Central Powers on railways meant that strategy, mobilization, and deployment of armies became connected in a way that was much more direct and rigid than had been the general experience. World War I was accordingly the most comprehensively planned in history, "not only thought, written, and talked about in general, but specifically laid out on paper in complex timetables, mobilization charts, and plans for men, weapons, and supplies. These plans were then practiced through war games, staff rides, and large-scale maneuvers before the war itself was declared."[38] This preplanning lasted not for days, weeks, or months, but for decades. In this context, the role of operational art was necessarily constrained by the framework of the campaign plan which was itself inextricably enmeshed in, and the product of, the processes of mobilization and strategic deployment.

The reliance on railways had another important impact. The bureaucratization of war had been driven by the progressive expansion of armies. That bureaucratization now expanded from the relatively narrow confines of the military staff and increasingly encompassed the agencies responsible for management of railways and telegraphs. Probably for the first time, interagency coordination became fundamental to the prosecution of war. While we see this now as "new" in the contemporary context, it has been an instrument of wars of national survival for at least a century.

For Germany, the challenge presented by this moment in the evolution of warfare received extra spice because, since the departure of Bismarck in 1890, German diplomacy had antagonized her neighbors and alarmed other more remote onlookers to such an extent that the country was now encircled by hostile alliances. German planning was therefore predicated on the inevitability of a war on two fronts, on each of which it would face an enemy of comparable power.

France had a modern railway system with major lines radiating from Paris. The Russian system was poor, very patchy, and incomplete. The German system reflected the federal nature of the new German State but was a little advanced over that of its competitors and had been somewhat influenced by military needs from its inception. In 1893 the German General Staff had assumed a measure of control over the building of track and the purchasing of equipment.[39] It was anticipated that, due to its better railway system, France would mobilize faster than the Russians, that France would begin an offensive as mobilization made troops available, and that this offensive would be in the "center," i.e., in Alsace and Lorraine. Consequently, German war planning anticipated a rapid war of annihilation against the French involving a holding action in the center while riposting with a massive envelopment around their western flank intended to effectively encircle the entirety of the French army. Once France was destroyed, forces would be rapidly switched to the Eastern Front to defeat the Russians.

The German war plan, of which the "Schlieffen Plan" was a part, connected the strategic, political, and economic circumstances of Germany with the conduct of a continent-wide war conducted in a number of noncontiguous theaters. It was produced and managed by supreme headquarters and clearly transcended classification as "operational" or as "a succession of tactical actions sharing some unifying idea within a portion of campaign." As such, the plan exemplified an activity which occurs definitionally and functionally at a higher level. In fact, it exemplifies strategy as expressed in the form of a number of campaign plans. The required coordination between German government agencies—diplomatic, telegraphic, and transport, the decision to breach Belgian neutrality, and the

coordination of complementary but discrete operations by different armies, each answering to supreme
headquarters, is clearly at a higher level than
"operational." The part of the strategic war plan that
dealt with the Western Front framed the campaigns
there by describing the operations that were to be
undertaken and allocating resources, objectives, and
milestones down to army level within each. Within
each of these operations, in the absence of an army
group level of command, each of the army commanders
sequenced his tactical actions to meet the demands of the
war plan. Operational art, although not yet recognized
by name, looked to achieve by tactical action what had
been proposed by strategy. It was 100 percent tactically
focused because it was undertaken within a campaign
context that had been entirely provided by strategy.

Theory as Praxis: *Freie Operationen.*

Apart from their interest in Clausewitz, admittedly
an important exception, the Germans have not been
active military theoreticians. Their predilection to
view war as an organic whole constantly undergoing
fundamental and comprehensive change, usually
for the worse, rested on a *Weltanschauung* heavily
influenced by romanticism, with a consequent lack of
desire to entomb the theory of war in an enlightenment
framework of definition, disaggregation, and analysis.
This is why Clausewitz, for example, concentrates on
the dynamics causing change rather than on producing
a taxonomy of all its manifestations. Moltke, with his
dictum that strategy was a system of expedients, was
not making excuses for a failure to plan, but rather was
accepting the infinite variety of circumstances that may
eventually have to be accommodated. The German

approach to warfare was therefore based on careful preparation of the individual with the understanding that, faced with situations of great novelty and fearsome prospect, only the man on the spot could hope to take actions that were actually appropriate. This is the origin of *auftragstaktik*, which the Anglophone world has taken up as "Mission Command" or "Directive Control" and which is aimed at creating sufficient scope for commanders at all levels to take actions based on their understanding of how their guiding purpose may be attained in the face of existing circumstances.

The term *"freie operationen"* or "free operations" entered German doctrine in 1996 to extend the concept of *auftragstaktik* into general application. According to Dieter Brand, it was a traditional idea which had been the antecedent and conceptual underpinning to *auftragstaktik* but which had previously existed only in practice and not in doctrine.[40] Its roots are easily seen in Frederick the Great's famous saying qualifying the need to obey orders absolutely and in Moltke's various aphorisms concerning the need to adapt to local conditions. *Freie operationen* were intended to enable creativity and flexible adaptation to local circumstances while retaining a focus on the outcome being sought. To sustain coherence in the face of complex and dynamic events, the Germans aimed not to control the individual actions of its soldiers, but to prepare them so that their commanders could confidently expect them to take the "right" actions. To this end, the German General Staff, with its rigorous procedures for officer selection and education and its system of staff rides, wargames, map exercises, and large-scale exercises with troops, has historically sought to provide commonality of approach and a measure of consistency to decisionmaking. Assigning general staff officers as chiefs of staff for commanders selected for their qualities of leadership, energy, and aggressiveness was intended to provide the capacity for *freie operationen* while keeping them firmly harnessed to the higher purpose—the annihilation of the enemy.

The exercise of *freie operationen* is well demonstrated by General Alexander von Kluck, commander of the most westerly German Army in the early stages of World War I. Although he had been a keen adherent of the need for the widest possible envelopment of the French Army, as the campaign in Belgium and northern France developed he came to the conclusion that, rather than continuing with the plan and moving to the west and south of Paris, the best opportunity to meet the guiding purpose—the annihilation of the French Army—required that he shorten his arc to sweep to the north and east of Paris. This was the "correct" solution given the circumstances as von Kluck saw them, and it was within his authority to make these adjustments. Although he didn't know it, von Kluck was demonstrating operational art. Faced with his initiative, supreme headquarters then, of course, had the role of either redirecting von Kluck or making the necessary adjustments to the rest of the theater. It chose the latter.[41] The determination of the Germans to provide scope for creativity and innovation is exemplified by the idea of *freie operationen*, is innate to their approach to warfare, and explains the relative (to the Russians, for example) scantiness of their operational doctrine or theory. To understand German operational art requires that one examine praxis rather than theory.

It is not necessary here to chart the entire course of World War I, but it presented in stark relief the twin-headed problem with which theory would henceforth have to deal. That is, on one hand nation-states were demonstrably not easily defeated in single decisive battles or even operations, while on the other hand, because of their power and organization, they were liable to field armies of size sufficient to enable the establishment of a defensive line with practically unassailable flanks—leading to the type of stabilized front seen in France and Belgium from 1914. This situation was the principal influence on the evolution of operational art in Germany between the wars.

Blitzkrieg: Penetration, Encirclement, Annihilation.

Germany's fundamental strategic problem of managing a potential two-front war had not changed. This meant that a rapid victory on at least one of those fronts was necessary for national survival. Therefore, short and violent wars aimed at the annihilation of at least one of the enemy armies continued to be seen as necessary. This was not new—at least since Moltke, the "annihilation principle" (*Vernichtungsprinzip*) had been the bedrock of German warfighting thought aditional view was that annihilation of an enemy required wide envelopment. This meant that the basic forms of maneuver seen early in World War I—frontal pressure paired with envelopment to enable the encirclement and destruction of an enemy—remained central to German thinking:

> Victory was seen to lie in strategic surprise, in the concentration of force at the decisive point, and in fast, far-reaching concentric encircling movements, all of which aimed at creating the decisive *Kesselschlachten* (cauldron battles) to surround, kill, and capture the opposing army in as short a time as possible.[42]

The objective of envelopment was not the flanks of the enemy but his line of retreat, the thinking being that this would force the enemy to fight with severed lines of communication and with a reversed front, leading most probably to disintegration and collapse. These aspects represented enduring themes in the German approach to warfare since Frederick the Great. As Matthew Cooper points out, "Double envelopment became their theme, *vernichtungsgedanke* their watchword."[43]

The realization of these traditional approaches in the face of a rapidly evolving technological environment had been the principal problem presented by World War I. To restore opportunities for envelopment and annihilation, tactical innovation was needed if the stabilized front was to be penetrated. The tactical failures of the war had begun to be remedied by its conclusion, and storm troop tactics had demonstrated that penetration of a fully-developed defensive zone was possible if small agile groups could be provided with sufficient striking power. The problem demonstrated during the Saint-Mihiel Offensive (April-September 1918), however, was that these groups lacked the endurance and mobility to turn their local tactical success into something more significant. Here the German experience countering Allied tanks was instructive. Tanks seemingly offered the ability to take the fundamentals of storm troop tactics and sustain them through the depth of the defended zone and into the undefended territory beyond. At the same time, the problems of sustaining artillery support beyond the initial range of the guns was to be countered by the use of aircraft in close support of the attacking forces. To maintain the speed of penetration necessary to offset the movement of defending forces to the point of penetration, the offensive would flow around centers of resistance, relying on follow-on forces to consolidate and sustain the gap created.

The Germans in the interwar years did not, as far as can be determined, recognize the term "operational art." The independence that commanders enjoyed under *freie operationen* to sequence tactical actions in pursuit of higher-level objectives meant that the role that we currently ascribe to operational art existed in the broad fabric of the German understanding of war and consequently in their preparation of leaders and training of staffs. World War II German operational art was therefore seen in praxis rather than in doctrine. Advanced combined arms tactics applied by aggressive leaders sometimes exercising considerable personal initiative to create and develop deep penetrations, followed by wide envelopments to encircle, isolate, and destroy large enemy groupings, was the German way of war. It was shared by the German military in a sufficiently broad sense apparently that it did not warrant comprehensive theoretical examination. The contribution of German theorists following World War I was therefore not in operational art, but in the development of an approach to combined arms tactics that was startlingly effective and which closely fitted the requirements of the German way of war. The employment of these combined arms tactics to execute annihilating cauldron battles came to be known in the Anglophone world as "Blitzkrieg." The execution of Blitzkrieg in attacks on France and Russia, in turn, demonstrated both its power and its limitations.

The evolution of the German plan to invade France, *Fall Gelb* (*Case Yellow*), is well known, but for the purposes of this monograph it is important for us to try to identify what in the plan is and is not operational art. As has been stated, the Germans during World War II did not recognize an operational level of war, an operational level of command, or the idea of operational art. The design of the campaign in France necessarily combined problems of tactics — e.g., the ability to move mechanized forces through the Ardennes and the penetration of the defense at Sedan, with problems of large-scale maneuver by multiple army groups; strategic problems of mobilization and the allocation of effort to other active fronts (such as the invasion of Norway); and strategic questions of how to bring about the submission of the French and possibly the British. If this process of designing a campaign is considered to be "operational art," then the term is certainly a very broad tent. In this case, encompassing all the headquarters from the head of state down to at least corps, at which level Guderian, for example, was clearly demonstrating operational art by conceiving and executing a succession of tactical actions to achieve the objectives laid down in the campaign plan.[44] This all-encompassing view of operational art is theoretically and doctrinally worthless because, in practice, it makes "operational art" nearly synonymous with "warfare" itself.

Alternatively, and more correctly, the design of the campaign in France was a strategic process in which the conversation between strategic aspirations and tactical possibilities was kept clearly in mind. France represented a single theater of operations, and from the start it was conceived that the single campaign to defeat the French would be conducted in a number of phases. The initial phase involved the coordination of the actions of German Army Group B in the low countries, A in the Ardennes, and C in Alsace. It was planned and commanded by the German supreme command including Hitler and his immediate advisers.

Having arrived at a scheme of maneuver and identified objectives down to army level and lower, allocated resources accordingly, and set key timings, the supreme headquarters then coordinated the conduct of the campaign day by day.

It can be understood as the establishment of three consecutive thrusts, only the first of which was clearly identified at the outset:

- The first flowed from three coordinated operations to apply frontal pressure in Belgium and the Netherlands and to penetrate the Maginot Line at Sedan, leading to the encirclement of the British Expeditionary Force (BEF) and the French 1st Army group in the Low Countries and the establishment of a new front roughly along the line of the Somme.

- With this first thrust successful, the subsequent phase of the campaign, which was not clearly envisaged at the start, involved penetrations of this new front to initiate:
  - a single operation to encircle the French 2nd Army Group and press it against the Atlantic coast, and
  - a further single operation that pressed the 3rd Army Group against the Vosge Mountains and the German frontier.

In practice, therefore, the German campaign in France was a product of strategy, with each of the headquarters further down the chain pursuing that strategy as it evolved in line with circumstances but with a gradually increasing focus on tactical realities. It is at the army group level and below that we most clearly see "operations" consisting of a sequence of tactical actions sharing a common purpose, with Guderian at and after Sedan providing the prime example.

The interplay of strategy and operational art is further demonstrated in the German invasion of Russia in late June 1941. In his memoir, Erich von Manstein sketches the debate that occurred over the plan as a whole.[45] According to him, the Army preferred a single thrust directed on Moscow, arguing that the Russians were obliged to defend it and therefore that is where their army could be forced to give battle. Once the Russian army was defeated, the political and economic objectives of the invasion would be more readily harvested. Adolph Hitler, however, sought to move directly on Leningrad, the birthplace of Bolshevism, and only subsequently on Moscow and the Ukraine.

The wisdom of this argument, or the lack of it, remains conjectural; whether the loss of Leningrad and/or Moscow and/or the Ukraine would really have broken the Russian will or ability to resist is not certain, although Moscow's role as the railway hub joining the South and East with the North and West seems to endow it with considerable military importance. Its capture would have substantially reduced the capacity of the Russians to shift defensive effort from place to place. In the end, Hitler's view prevailed, with the capture of Leningrad, over 800 kilometers from the German line of departure, becoming the immediate objective. To avoid the paralyzing prospect of a stabilized front, it was believed necessary, before moving on to Leningrad, to destroy the mass of the Russian army, thought at the time to comprise somewhere around 147 available divisions (although by August 11, 1941, the Germans had encountered 360) before it could withdraw from western Russia. The resulting campaign plan envisaged an offensive on a broad front with two army groups directed to pin Russian forces in White Russia against the Baltic and subsequently destroy them, and a third to encircle and destroy Russian forces in the Western Ukraine. Following success in this phase, subsequent phases of the campaign would be devoted to the seizure of Moscow and the Eastern Ukraine.[46]

Following the usual collaborative planning effort, the strategic directive for Operation BARBAROSSA, prepared by supreme headquarters (*Oberkommando der Wehrmacht* [OKW]) and signed by Hitler, describes the campaign in some detail.[47] It allocates two Army groups to the area north of the Pripyat Marshes and describes their broad maneuver and objectives. The single army group south of the Pripyat Marshes is directed to conduct a double envelopment, with one wing originating near Lublin and directed at Kiev and the other originating in southern Rumania. Following in the wake of this directive, the Army High Command (*Oberkommando des Heeres* [OKH]) issued its own directive providing details of the organization of each of the Army Groups, plus their start positions, axes of advance, and immediate and subsequent objectives. These two directives, which comprise the campaign design, are products of a strategic process simultaneously considering ends, ways, and means. For the Germans at least, campaign planning was a task for strategy.

Within this broad front, the German way of war was successfully demonstrated through the customary combination of frontal pressure with deep penetrations to establish annihilating killing grounds. Within the classical definition of an operation, provided earlier, the establishment and prosecution of each of these huge actions was an operation demonstrating operational art in its own right and depending on the freedom of action available to the commander. If he were really free to sequence tactical actions as he saw fit, each of the wings of the envelopment could also arguably be considered operational art. If this view is taken, operational art has an overwhelmingly tactical focus, and its role is considerably clarified. The campaign plan, provided by strategy, provides objectives, axes, resources, and timings to operational commanders who then conduct the sequence of tactical actions necessary to comply with it. Good operational art in this context is principally tactical and is largely concerned with meeting the objectives provided by the campaign plan in the most efficient and elegant manner possible. Its economy is designed to avoid unproductive tactical encounters, creating opportunities for more productive ones and exploiting the situations that emerge from each engagement, whether successful or unsuccessful. Accordingly, operational art is, or should be, much more about tactics than about strategy.

By the end of September 1941, the Germans believed they had inflicted losses on the Russians amounting to two and a half million men, 22,000 guns, 18,000 tanks, and 14, 000 aircraft.[48] By the end of 1941, Russian losses of men had grown to 4 million killed and three and a half million taken prisoner. The seven great encounters of Bialystok-Misnk, Smolensk, Uman, Gomel, Kiev, The Sea of Azov, and Bryansk-Vyazma alone resulted in the capture of more then two and a quarter million soldiers and the destruction or capture of 9,327 tanks and 16,179 guns. In a further 13 minor battles of encirclement, another 736,000 Soviet soldiers were taken prisoner, while 4,960 tanks and 9,033 guns were captured or destroyed.[49] Despite these huge losses, Russia was not defeated. However, it is hard to argue this was the result of a failure of German operational art, which did demonstrably lead to the wholesale slaughter of the enemy. Rather, the failure here was one of strategy — poor strategy that led the Germans to design campaigns with objectives that were too ambitious to be achieved by the tactical resources they were able to allocate and apply.

German operational art in World War II was traditional rather than revolutionary. It rested on the use of the advanced combined arms tactics that emerged from their analysis of the lessons of World War I, involving the traditional combination of frontal pressure with deep penetration leading to encirclement and annihilation. German operational art was reliably successful because the preparation of German commanders and staff officers, and the tactical excellence of the Wehrmacht, underpinned the flexible and adaptive implementation of ambitious schemes of maneuver. Without sound strategy, however, operational art is helpless, and in the German case strategy was too often flawed.

OPERATIONAL ART GETS A NAME: TUKHACHEVSKIY AND DEEP ATTACKS

At the risk of leaping a little ahead, it is necessary to explain the wider Soviet conceptual framework before plotting the evolution of operational art in Russia. It was the Soviets who gave us the term operational art. Although the term "operation" in its special meaning of a sequenced group of tactical actions had been around since the second half of the 19th century, the identification and codification of operational art had to await the arrival of the socialist state. In stark contrast to the German "war as a whole" idea, the Soviets, guided by dialectical Marxism, found it necessary to distill "science" out of the universal experience of war, in the process producing a comprehensive and multi-partite taxonomy of its components.[50] In Soviet usage, military science was understood as a system of knowledge facilitating the understanding of practical experience rather than some concept of incontestable precision. The military art, as a subset of military science, involved the application of this system of knowledge in practical situations.[51] **Operational art, a subset of military art, employed tactics and logistics to resolve a series of tactical problems that together were intended to achieve an intermediate aim within a campaign.**

In the wake of Russia's failure against the Germans in World War I, the Bolshevik Revolution of November 1917 against the Czarist government would eventually see the establishment of the USSR. The ensuing civil war (1917-23) led to an oft-unnoticed concurrent war against Poland (1919-21). In combination with the application of Marxist ideology to the problem of armed struggle, the lessons of these three wars shaped the development of Soviet military theory. It is worth noting from the start that Soviet theory was firmly rooted in a specific strategic context—it was intended to resolve the problems attendant on defending the Soviet state against a threat from Western Europe. Therefore, the locale and belligerents of the future war for which they were preparing were already largely decided, and the initial debates within the Soviet Union were focused on the form that the war should take. Accordingly,

> M. V. Frunze, M. N. Tukhachevskiy, A. I. Yegorov, V. K. Triandafillov, . . . N. Ye.Varfolomeyev, and others were in favour of developing a theory of operations for a concrete war in defence of the only soviet state in the world. In their opinion this theory would serve as the foundation of a specific system for conducting operations and a guide specifically for the Red Army.[52]

It is not necessary to recount the entirety of the debate here, but initially it involved a dispute between A. A. Svechin and M. Tukhachevskiy over whether an offensive or defensive war was most appropriate in view of the threat to, and the level of industrial and economic development of, the tyro state. In the end, Tukhachevskiy's view was to prevail, and Soviet doctrine broke with historical Russian practice and settled on an approach to defensive war that rested heavily on offensive action.[53] As with the Germans, the Soviet approach to war would be to seek the annihilation of the enemy, rather than his exhaustion.[54]

As well as gaining broad command experience during the Civil War, Tukhachevskiy had been the (defeated) commander of the Northern Front during the climactic Battle of Warsaw in the war against Poland, and this experience shaped his understanding of the problems of contemporary war. A number of things had gone wrong. Tukhachevskiy had relied on the moral impact of his advance to break the Polish will to resist and therefore had focused on geographic objectives rather than on the destruction of Polish forces. As a result, despite a succession of tactical setbacks, the Polish forces remained largely intact, and, although their line was pushed back, the Russians could not seize Warsaw before they themselves culminated. At the same time, the Southern Front, swinging around the Pripyet Marshes, failed to coordinate with the Northern Front, with the consequence that the Polish line was not suppressed along its entire length. This enabled troops to be withdrawn from unpressured parts of the Polish line to form a counterattack force sufficiently powerful to throw back and decisively defeat the Russians.

Soviet Operational Art: Penetration, Encirclement, Annihilation.

In combination with the lessons of World War I—principally the problems of penetrating an intact front that had no assailable flanks and the demonstrated difficulty of defeating a nation-state—the lessons of Warsaw had a profound effect on Russian theory. The problem of the stabilized front that had been so amply demonstrated in World War I was the fundamental challenge to be resolved. Initially the debate was how this eventuality could be avoided, but quickly it was accepted that any sound basis for the development of theory should accept that such a front would occur, and that solutions should aim to deal with it. The need for a series of repeated blows to defeat the mass army of a contemporary state was already well-established in military thought. The challenge was to combine the two contradictory problems of an intact and defensively strong stabilized front with a strategy of annihilation, but without repeating the bloody stalemate of the Western Front in World War I.

Tukhachevskiy immediately understood that if the Red Army were to successfully resolve this contradiction, certain operational questions would have to be addressed first. "It was the demand to solve the problem of annihilation that led Tukhachevskiy and his colleagues to a rigorous and thorough examination of operational art."[55] By 1923 Tukhachevskiy had begun to articulate the broad shape of Soviet operational art:

> [S]ince it is impossible, with the extended fronts of modern times, to destroy the enemy's army at a single blow, we are obligated to try to do this gradually by operations which will be more costly to the enemy than to ourselves. . . . In short, a series of destructive

operations conducted on logical principles and linked together by an uninterrupted pursuit may take the place of the decisive battle that was the form of engagement in the armies of the past, which fought on shorter fronts.[56]

This was not intended to be a Fullerian lunge for the jugular of the opposing army nor an attempt to paralyze it through fear. Tukhachevskiy and his colleagues were intent on physical annihilation. This was because, one suspects, Tukhachevskiy had tried the "moral factors" approach at Warsaw, and it had not worked. As a result, Tukhachevskiy was quite clear that "an operation is the organized struggle of each of the armies for the destruction of the men and material of the other. Not the destruction of some hypothetical, abstract nervous system of the army, but destruction of the real organism—the troops and real nervous system of the opponent, the army's communications, must be the operational goal."[57] The difference between this focus and the approaches advanced in the recent era of network-centric euphoria, for example, is noteworthy. It is further developed in the discussion of "strategic paralysis" and "operational shock" in the next section.

We may encapsulate the two dominant streams in Russian operational art as follows: **successive operations**, the infliction of a series of damaging blows, along with **deep operations**, with the linking of these blows designed to achieve penetrations of increasing depth until the enemy defensive zone, including deep reserves, had been pierced and the conditions for mobile warfare thereby reestablished. These preparations would create the conditions for the encirclement and subsequent annihilation of large enemy groups.[58] These two ideas were eventually combined in Soviet deep operations theory in which a deep attack was understood as simultaneously destroying, suppressing, and pinning down not only those defending forces designated to repel an attack from the front, but also those located well behind the front. In practice, this would mean

> a significant penetration into the tactical depth of the enemy disposition; [then] immediate infliction of a second, third, and subsequent blows on the heels of the first [in order to] bring the enemy to complete defeat. The ideal would be to plan the actions of friendly armed forces in such a way that, employing a series of crushing blows carried to their conclusion, they would lead to a complete defeat of the enemy, to his complete capitulation.[59]

Although deep attack theory well matched the nature of the problem, how the deep attack could be reliably conducted was a puzzle that had occupied planners on the western front throughout World War I. Taken as a whole, technological developments had favored the defense. However, the tank, aircraft, and radio communications meant that technology came to favor the offense once a penetration had been achieved, specifically by enabling its development into depth at a speed that could thwart enemy attempts at defensive maneuver. Therefore, to be successful, the deep attack needed to achieve the initial penetration, suppress the rest of the enemy defensive system so as to provide time for the initial exploitation of the penetration to gather steam, and then be able to follow up that initial exploitation to expand and support it, bringing about a collapse of the defensive front.

By 1928 this thinking had become officially accepted, and the Russian General Staff decreed: "It is essential to conduct a series of successive operations which are appropriately distributed in space and time. By the combination of a series of operations, it is essential to force the enemy to exhaust its material and human resources or to cause the enemy to accept battle by its main mass of armed troops under disadvantageous conditions and eliminate them."[60] By 1936 the deep attack was written into Field Service Regulations. It would take place in the campaign context of a general offensive intended to engage the entirety of the enemy defensive front to suppress its ability to respond with large-scale maneuver. It was thus described as a four-echelon offensive:[61]

- Air instruments were considered to be the first echelon, intended to achieve control of the air and begin attacks on identified targets;
- The second echelon was comprised of combined arms "shock" armies with lavish allocations of artillery intended to break into and through the enemy's defensive crust; these shock armies were themselves deeply echeloned so as to achieve an overwhelming change in the correlation of forces along the axes chosen for the breakthrough;
- In the third echelon, mobile groups comprising large formations of tanks supported by parachute troops would develop the penetration to its full depth; and,
- The fourth echelon, essentially a reserve, would lend weight to the advance and consolidate gains.

With the occasional minor modification to accommodate technological innovation, especially the advent of nuclear weapons and the opportunities offered by rotary wing aircraft, this broad approach to the deep attack was sustained in Soviet doctrine until the collapse of the USSR and the end of the Cold War in 1989.[62]

The evolution of the theory of the deep attack took place in conjunction with a refinement in Soviet understanding of operations and operational art. Because single decisive battles were no longer expected, the path to the achievement of the annihilation of the enemy needed to be broken into a series of operations. Operations were understood as a sequence of tactical actions

> directed towards the achievement of a certain intermed-
> iate goal in a certain theater of military operations. . . . On
> the basis of the goal of an operation, operational art sets
> forth a whole series of tactical missions . . .[and] dictates
> the basic line of conduct of an operation, depending on
> the material available, the time which may be allotted
> for the handling of different tactical missions, the forces
> which may be deployed . . . and finally the nature of the
> operation itself.[63]

In this formation there is a clear hierarchy of responsibilities, but not an articulation of a *"level"* distinct from tactics. Supreme headquarters frames the campaign, that is, it defines the theater, sets objectives, and allocates resources. Within this framework, the front (army group equivalent) decides on the successive operations necessary to achieve the campaign objectives.[64] In today's terminology, then, it is the task first of the national headquarters and subsequently of the theater commanders to establish the framework within which individual operations are to be conducted. Strategy, to the Soviets, was "the art of combining preparation for war and a grouping of operations to achieve the aim put forth for war for the armed forces,"[65] that is, strategy designed campaigns and decided which operations were to be conducted.

It is within each of the successive operations laid down by strategy that operational art comes into play.

Since the realities of the theater and logistics meant that the operational potential of any force is limited, the Soviet response was to seek to make each operation decisive within its own depth. That is, each of the successive operations was intended to annihilate the enemy within its allocated geographic area by means of breakthroughs and encirclements.[66] According to Isserson, "The core problem of operational art was **the conduct of the individual operation** involving the unification in time and space, both frontally and in depth, of separate combat efforts, . . . not directly connected tactically, to achieve an overall assigned aim."[67]

It is not useful to try to separate the Soviet understanding of operational art from the concept of deep attack. The deep attack was an operational technique intended to be applied by operational art. The two conceptual systems co-evolved and progressively grew into a kind of unity in which the Soviet theory of operational art came to describe how deep attack might be employed, while deep attack defined the limits of soviet operational art. For our purposes, however, the key points are that Soviet operational theory and the deep attack are **specific** solutions to a problem set defined by the unique geopolitical circumstances of the USSR, that is, they were solutions to the specific problems posed by mass armies fielded by nation-states threatening the Soviet state. As a result, they were intended to deal with the challenges of a stabilized front and the difficulties of defeating states. Equally, the Soviets who gave us the term operational art also provided it with a very clear parameter—strategy. It was strategy, expressed in a campaign plan, that defined the operations to be conducted and the operational art which conducted them. The operational objectives as provided by strategy were made clear, and operational art had merely to arrange matters for their achievement.

THE BRITISH SCHOOL: BLOODLESS WAR AND "STRATEGIC PARALYSIS"

Unsurprisingly, the British approach to warfare is conditioned by the nation's history. Relatively secure on their moated island, the British have traditionally committed modest land forces to European wars in order to cement alliances and demonstrate commitment rather than to seek decisive victory in their own right. Therefore, the British generally have not themselves sought the complete overthrow of their enemies and have seen most wars as "limited" in both the ends that were reasonably attainable and the degree of commitment made to them. This "limited liability" approach is culturally reinforced by a history of imperial policing and a strong navalist tradition. Naval warfare is seldom decisive in itself; Trafalgar did not defeat Napoleon, and victory over the armada did not defeat Spain. Naval victory in both cases prevented the enemy from setting the conditions for a decisive battle on land. In broad, British military history has not been shaped by unlimited commitments in pursuit of unlimited objectives. This cultural foundation has shaped the evolution of British theory.

George Orwell noted that "there is something unsatisfactory in tracing an historical change to an individual theorist, because a theory does not gain ground unless material conditions favor it." This insight is especially true of the evolution of operational art between the world wars.[68] The fresh experience of

49

World War I was both shared and compelling. Inevitably there was an awareness by those working in the field of what others were doing internationally and thus a degree of cross-fertilization. It is fair to say, however, that generally the extent to which any one country was directly influenced by what was being written or done in another was peripheral. The theorists working in each country were necessarily compelled to work within the context presented by their own specific circumstances. The Germans, for example, were not greatly influenced by the Russians nor vice versa. With each faced with a common problem and a common set of technologies, however, a degree of convergence did emerge between them, with the approaches to operational art in both countries coming to rest on frontal pressure, deep penetration, encirclement, and annihilation.[69]

Importantly, neither J. F. C. Fuller nor B. H. Liddell-Hart were the progenitors of Blitzkreig, nor were they more than marginally influential in the development of Russian theory. The historiography of Liddell-Hart's claim to a role in the birth of Blitzkreig has been comprehensively covered and is not important here. A quick look at publication dates suggests that the Russians were already well on the way by the time Fuller produced his major works and were nigh complete by the arrival of Liddell-Hart's contributions.[70] Equally, neither Fuller nor Liddell-Hart was sufficiently influential to engender genuine change in British doctrine or practice at the time.

Nonetheless, despite failing to make the leap from theory to praxis in any country between the wars, the contributions of both Fuller and Liddell-Hart are of interest because of the extent to which they contrast with each other and, in particular, with the Germans and Russians. To some extent, these contrasts are at least partially concealed beneath superficial similarities;

again, these similarities make comparisons instructive and, importantly, provide a conceptual bridge to more contemporary experience.

Although both Fuller and Liddell-Hart had a deep grounding in military history, it was the vivid experience of World War I that was most influential in the development of their thinking. Thus, along with the Russians and Germans, the problems of dealing with the stabilized front and the apparent tactical superiority of the defense provided their focus.

J. F. C. Fuller and "Strategic Paralysis."

Fuller had remained an active soldier throughout the war and was an early recruit to the emerging tank arm. As a result, his theoretical contribution, at least initially, centerd on how tanks could be exploited to restore the power of the tactical offensive. Perhaps because he had risen to relatively senior ranks and had been responsible for the planning of battles (including the battle of Cambrai in November 1917), he was not overly adverse to the ugly realities of battle and was inclined to accept that fighting was a necessary and inescapable part of war. Despite this, both he and Liddell-Hart sought to find a way to fight that directly minimized casualties—they sought a way of war that was, if not bloodless, at least humane. Fuller and Liddell-Hart's cultural context—British history—was able to accommodate this nuanced approach. It, however, created a chasm between the Europeans and the British school that could not be bridged. Since Napoleon, the Europeans had viewed war as a fight for national survival—in the face of such apocalyptic ends, constraining the expenditure of blood or treasure was nonsensical. Bloodless war was not a notion that strongly impressed itself on European theorists.

Beginning with his **Plan 1919,** written in May 1918, Fuller described how tanks, supported by gas bombardment, could penetrate the tactical defense and throw themselves over the communications of the enemy army and in particular at enemy headquarters to destroy or capture these "centers of thought." The result would be to paralyze the enemy's ability to conduct defensive maneuver. Under cover of this "strategic paralysis" brought about by the "barrage of demoralization," the main attack would begin the piecemeal destruction of the enemy's main forces — its infantry and artillery.[71] The differences between Fuller and his continental contemporaries are clear. Although both sought the demoralization of the enemy, the latter wanted to carry the main battle into depth to force the enemy to fight at a marked disadvantage with a reversed front, whereas Fuller saw the main battle being conducted along the original front, albeit under conditions made more favorable to the attacker because of the paralysis of the enemy command apparatus.

To Fuller, the moral effect of the deep attack was crucial, to the Europeans the deep attack was a step on the path to the physical destruction of the enemy, and the moral effect was an added bonus. That Tukhachevskiy was aware of, but rejected, Fuller's thesis is clear from the Russian's comment that

> an operation is the organized struggle of each of the armies for the destruction of the men and material of the other. Not the destruction of some hypothetical, abstract nervous system of the army, but destruction of the real organism — the troops and real nervous system of the opponent, the army's communications, must be the operational goal.[72]

Similarly, German *kesselschlacht* was aimed not at the demoralization of the enemy but at forcing him to fight with a reversed front and preventing him from escaping annihilation—the fact that this often also demoralized him only made a little easier the battle to destroy those entrapped.

Liddell-Hart and War on the Mind.

Liddell-Hart, on the other hand, had been wounded in 1916 and took no further part in subsequent combat operations. He had initially approached the war with enthusiasm and commitment, and it was only in the postwar years that he began to take a more jaundiced view of its conduct. Apparently, over a quarter of his high school graduating class, together with a commensurate portion of the rest of the "flower of English youth," were killed in the war, and the extent of the effort swept away the old social and economic order by which Liddell-Hart had been formed. Possibly as a result of this, he was particularly keen to find a way to avoid the carnage that he had experienced firsthand and consistently sought to describe how battle might be avoided.

In his writings, Liddell-Hart often uses the term "strategy" when he is in fact (in stark contrast to Clausewitz and others) speaking about operational art. He coined the term "grand strategy" to fill the resulting void in the higher direction of wars. To Liddell-Hart, "tactics lies in and fills the province of fighting. [Operational art] not only stops on the frontier, but has for its purpose the reduction of fighting to the slenderest possible proportions." This statement is unobjectionable, for in seeking to reduce the fighting as much as possible, Liddell-Hart is providing one reasonable parameter of "good" operational art. He accepts that a decisive battle may still be necessary, but argues that good operational art should ensure that it be fought under the most advantageous circumstances possible. "The more advantageous the circumstances, the less, proportionately, will be the fighting. The perfection of [operational art] therefore would be to produce a decision without any serious fighting."[73]

Liddell-Hart used the term "dislocation" of the enemy to describe the creation of a situation that is "so advantageous that if it does not cause the collapse of the enemy of itself — its continuation by battle is sure to do so." Physical dislocation he describes as a move that upsets the enemy's dispositions and, by compelling a sudden change of front, disrupts the distribution and organization of his forces, separates his forces, endangers his supplies, or menaces his withdrawal routes.[74] He grants that these most often flow from a turning movement — from forcing the enemy to fight with a reversed front. Put simply, therefore, Liddell-Hart is telling us that turning the enemy confers substantial military advantage. The novelty of this conclusion is not compelling.

In the context of the problem of the stabilized front after World War I, the Germans and Russians attempted to develop techniques accepting that such a front existed and which were intended to deal with it. Liddell-Hart however sought to surprise the enemy by going around his flank along the "line of least expectation." If a stabilized front did, in fact, exist, he recognized that there might be a need to open an "inner flank" after local penetration.[75] But Liddell-Hart does not explain how this inner flank may be created and deepened sufficiently to pierce an enemy's defended zone and thus create the opportunity for mobile warfare. As a result, he is restating the problem of World War I rather than describing its solution.

Liddell-Hart was much taken by the achievements of the Mongols, by U.S. Civil War cavalry raiders, and by Sherman — particularly his march to Atlanta.[76] In analyzing the British mechanization experiments in the mid-1930s, he described his ideal of the operations of the tank brigade:

> The deeper behind the battle zone that the tank brigade could penetrate, the more widespread would be the confusion and dislocation it would cause, and the more effective would be its action. Moreover the deeper it went the safer it would be . . . it must therefore, move rapidly and be able to appear and disappear . . . It must . . . continually maneuver so as to threaten a number of objectives. It must induce enemy concentrations in one direction and then suddenly move 60 or 70 miles elsewhere. It must be able to strike rapidly, carrying out effective destruction in 2 or 3 hours and withdraw rapidly and leave the enemy uncertain of its exact whereabouts."[77]

Based on these models, he relentlessly preached logistic self-sufficiency, imagining a streamlined armored force carrying only the bare necessities, living off the countryside, and aided in critical moments by the delivery of essential supplies from the air.[78] To achieve his ideal, he was seeking a stripped down force that did not depend on its own lines of supply and was therefore entirely unencumbered in its swoop on the enemy's. This is a romantic notion of the operations of a mechanized raiding force rather than a practical prescription that can, or could then, be applied in practice. No large enemy force will be turned by the mere presence in its rear of a band of mechanized chindits. The turning effect flows not from irritation, but from the need to actually turn a large force to create a new front while simultaneously fighting on the original front and to sustain supply. The striking power and sustainability of the turning force is therefore of fundamental importance. Here, Liddell-Hart is too impressed by the emerging tactical power of the tank and too impressed by his reading of history. He therefore leans too far into the ideal and pays too little attention to realities.

As well as physical dislocation, Liddell-Hart put forward the idea of psychological dislocation. This he described as the effect on the enemy commander of being surprised and turned.[79] "The key to success . . . lies in rapidity of leverage, progressively extended deeper—in demoralising the opposition by creating successive flank threats quicker than the enemy can meet them, so that his resistance as a whole or in parts, is loosened by the fear of being cut off."[80] Psychological dislocation was, in Liddell-Hart's view, as powerful as its physical cousin.

Psychological dislocation and Fuller's "strategic paralysis," if not synonymous, then are at least closely related ideas that are worth more detailed examination since their starkly deliberate contrast with the Russian and German focus on annihilation raises important questions for the contemporary operational artist. This similarity will be discussed in more detail later.

Shimon Naveh and Operational Shock.

In 1996 Shimon Naveh, a retired Israeli general (and admittedly something of an adherent of the British School), published *In Pursuit of Military Excellence*.[81] In it he traces the evolution of the annihilation principle and argues, as does Liddell-Hart, that it is bankrupt. In its stead, he proposes the concept of operational shock, which is a restatement of Fuller's strategic paralysis and Liddell-Hart's psychological dislocation although Naveh wrongly attributes the idea to Russian innovation. Naveh quite rightly takes a systems view of warfare.[82] He describes operational shock as "disrupting the opposing system's rationale by removing command from the system."[83] This is clearly synonymous with Fuller's prescription (from 1919) to attack the enemy's "centers of thought" in order to create a "barrage of demoralization" that would make the piecemeal destruction of the enemy so much easier.

Two aspects of Soviet thought, in particular, attract Naveh's attention: recognition of the importance of the turning maneuver, and the Soviet emphasis, from about 1970, on simultaneity. The turning maneuver has already been discussed in detail, and its contribution to psychological dislocation and strategic paralysis is apparent. Naveh may be guilty of wishful thinking, however, in arguing that the Soviet embrace of turning maneuvers was either unique or, more importantly, focused on a psychological rather than physical outcome. The Soviet's way of war was based on a search for certainty through the application of overwhelming mass in a manner intended to annihilate the enemy.[84] Deep battle and successive operations described the techniques to be used to achieve this. The uncertain psychological advantages of encircling the enemy were clearly secondary to the physical certainties of killing him. Military adventurism was not a trait encouraged within the Soviet hierarchy.

Simultaneity is a little more complicated. From the lessons broached earlier from the Soviet-Polish war, the Soviets had recognized the need to suppress the enemy's ability to conduct defensive maneuver. In the 1920s, this had been primarily achieved by engaging the entire enemy front to tie down as many of his forces as possible. Over the succeeding decades, the increased range of indirect fire, the power of supporting aircraft, and the mobility of reserves meant that this suppressive effect had to be extended into greater depth. As a result, the use of air, long-range artillery, forward detachments, and mobile groups to disrupt the entire depth of the enemy's defended zone increased in importance. After World War II, this suppressive action was necessarily expanded to encompass nuclear delivery means and command and control. On this basis, it could be argued that the increasing importance of simultaneity was not predicated on a search for something new — "operational shock" — but rather represented a continuation of the fundamental mechanisms of Soviet operational art: frontal pressure and deep penetration leading to encirclement and annihilation, while making allowances for changes in the objective conditions of warfare.[85]

Despite the weaknesses identified here, there is much to be gained from reading Fuller, Liddell-Hart, and Naveh. Liddell-Hart, in particular, is able to exploit (perhaps torture) history to isolate lessons that excite and inform.[86] But in understanding the evolution of operational art, it is important to be quite clear that for Fuller, Liddell-Hart, and Naveh, demoralization was the aim of a deep attack, whereas for the Europeans, demoralization followed from the likelihood of annihilation and eased the path to it. In operational planning, there is a stark contrast between stunning an enemy into submission and killing him.[87]

FM 100-5 and the Leavenworth Heresy.

War and politics, campaign and statecraft, are Siamese twins, inseparable and interdependent; and to talk of military operations without the direction and interference of an administrator is as absurd as to plan a campaign without recruits, pay or rations.

Nicolay and Hay "Lincoln"[88]

So far as the situation in Iraq is concerned, the planning/strategy failures are legion: there was no plan to prevent looting, no plan for security/stabilization, no plan for running the country; bureaucratic warfare between the department of State and DoD over team personnel and other issues were not reined in by the National Security Council; Presidential Envoy Bremer's CPA and its predecessor "have been undermanned and operating with team B from the beginning," with no standby capacity and bodies having to be scrounged from the State Department: the international police, justice, and rule of law teams were never brought in; there was no planning for a stabilization force, there were not enough troops, and there was no mandate to perform stabilization tasks for what troops we had; the war was essentially continued throughout the reconstruction effort, with lack of security shutting down some contractor work; there is a lack of good intelligence; it is not clear to whom the government will be transferred, . . . public information/psyops needs fixing; lack of greater international involvement hurts the legitimacy of our effort.

Bathsheba Crocker
December 2004

Language is not simply a reporting device for experience but a defining framework for it.

Benjamin Whorf
"Thinking in Primitive Communities"

In 1982 the U.S. Army published a revised version of FM 100-5 which described how the U.S. Army intended to fight. The 1982 version formed a key component in the post-Vietnam renaissance that was sweeping through the U.S. Army at the time. The advent of the all-volunteer Army brought with it a renewal of military professionalism in the widest sense, and this flowed into approaches to training and education as well as how the U.S. Army, as an institution, viewed war and preparation for it.

One part of this new direction was a refocusing away from counterinsurgency towards the defense of the North Atlantic Treaty Organization (NATO) as being the Army's core activity. Improvements in technology were beginning to redress the absolute advantage conferred by mass, and the introduction of anti-tank guided weapons, night vision devices, and artillery submunitions were beginning to make the defeat of a Warsaw Pact offensive appear feasible even without recourse to nuclear weapons. In this environment, the 1982 version of FM 100-5 introduced Air-Land battle which described a joint approach to defeating Soviet operational art. Air-Land Battle sought to moderate the force ratios encountered in the close battle against the Soviets by "merging the Active Defense (the centerpiece of the 1976 version of FM 100-5) and deep attack of follow-on echelons into one battle."[89] Air-Land battle also introduced into American doctrine much of what we know as maneuver theory. To a large extent, at least for maneuver forces, it described a modernized Blitzkrieg seeking to exploit the capabilities offered by highly trained professional soldiers manning the superb new weapons systems, such as the Abrams main battle tank (MBT), Bradley infantry fighting vehicle (IFV), multiple launch rocket system (MLRS), and *Apache* attack helicopter that were then becoming available. All this was to take place in a framework provided by the customary U.S. excellence in logistics. This was well done and laudable. More importantly for our purposes, however, it introduced to the American Army the idea of the *operational level of war*.

It is not clear how the German view of war as a whole or the Soviet recognition of operational art became translated, in American usage, into a discrete level of war, existing somewhere between strategy and tactics, but the translation became the source of much subsequent confusion. This confusion is demonstrated in the single paragraph on pp. 2-3 of the 1982 manual that introduced this new species to the military menagerie:

> The Operational Level of War involves planning and conducting campaigns. Campaigns are sustained operations designed to defeat an enemy force in a specified place and time with simultaneous and sequential battles. The disposition of forces, selection of objectives, and actions to weaken or outmaneuver the enemy all set the terms for the next battle and exploit tactical gains. They are all part of the operational level of war.

Here FM 100-5 removes from strategy its traditional role of planning campaigns and conflates the term "campaign" with what the Soviets would recognize as an "operation"—a sequence of simultaneous and sequential battles, connected by a unifying idea and intended to defeat an enemy force. This original error was further compounded in the 1986 version of FM 100-5 when the term "operational art" was introduced to the American lexicon and defined as "the employment of military forces to attain strategic goals in a theater through the **design**, organization, and conduct of campaigns and major operations." This new and heretical understanding of operations and operational art spread through the Anglophone world like a virus. With minor variations in spelling, the same definitions had appeared in British, Canadian, and Australian doctrine by the early years of the 1990s where they remain relatively unchanged to this day.[90]

In seeking to understand the provenance of this new idea, a number of possibilities suggest themselves. As operational art was being born in English, its strategic context—the defense of NATO—had already been established; hence, the question of who, in fact, planned campaigns did not arise. The design of the campaign to defend NATO was already complete by 1982 and was not to change substantially between then and the fall of the Iron Curtain. Although the Supreme Allied Commander Europe (SACEUR) and his staff clearly had a role in campaign design, the probability that any conventional confrontation could escalate into nuclear conflagration and, even without nuclear weapons, that most of the members countries would be laid waste and their military and economic power substantially destroyed, necessarily engaged their national governments very intimately. The imperative to defend as far forward along the Inner German Border as possible, the likely Warsaw Pact axes and scheme of maneuver, the forces to be provided by each member country together with their responsibilities, areas of operations, limitations on employment, and even likely combat effectiveness, had all been factored into a unified military plan and agreed by the governments of the member countries.

The U.S. chain of command resulting from the Goldwater-Nichols Act had established the role of the combatant commanders in chief as joint warfighters in a chain of command connected with the President through the Secretary of Defense. Defining their role in the process of conducting a war necessarily involved defining their inputs and outputs. Thus the idea of an operational level of war charged with campaign planning met a bureaucratic need — establishment of jurisdictional definition among an influential group of senior officers — no bad thing if one is trying to get new doctrine agreed upon. In sum, then, it seems most likely that the idea of an operational level of war arose at least partially for bureaucratic reasons rather than reasons having to do with how to wage war.

There is nothing intrinsically erroneous with ascribing new meanings to existing terms — language formation is, after all, a dynamic process. Thus defining operational art in the way it was in the 1986 edition is not necessarily "wrong." However, in combination with the 1982 edition, the changes had the pernicious effect of perverting the original purpose of operational art — i.e., facilitating the dialogue between tactics and strategy — by creating a discrete and influential intermediate level of command, thus actually weakening and possibly muddling the tactical-strategic interface. More specifically, the misunderstanding of the role of operational art as proselytized in FM 100-5 and the creation of an "Operational Level of War" have led to an independent layer of command that has usurped the role of strategy and thereby resisted the role that the civilian leadership should play in campaign planning.

The Problem of Levels.

Arthur Lykke, in an influential article published in 1989, described strategy as consisting of **ends**, or objectives towards which one strives; **ways**, or courses of action; and **means**, or instruments by which some end can be achieved.[91] If we accept this construct, we reach the conclusion that strategy necessarily requires the simultaneous consideration of ends, ways, and means. In the case of a specific conflict, the choice of ways includes campaign design, i.e., the decisions on whom, where, and how to fight. Campaign design would also include a clear view on the scheme of maneuver, the operations that seem likely to be necessary, and therefore the resources required. Failure to complete, or errors in the completion of, this analysis risks seeking to achieve too much with too little or, conversely, incurring opportunity costs that might detract from the prosecution of the wider conflict.

Of equal importance, each individual campaign needs to be examined in the wider strategic context to ensure that the internal ends-ways-means rationale for it is in accord with the higher direction of national strategy and is likely to be politically sustainable through its planned duration. In this context, operations, as a sequence of tactical actions, and tactics, actual battles and engagements, clearly come under the category of "means." Observe that this analysis leads to a model broadly consonant with Scharnhorst's and Clausewitz's dictum that we consider war as a whole; apparently encapsulates the idea of war as a *Gestalt*; and offers opportunities for the multiple loops and connections that recognize war as a complex adaptive system. This model is also broadly in accord with theory and is entirely consonant with German and Soviet approaches to operational art. (See Figure 2.)

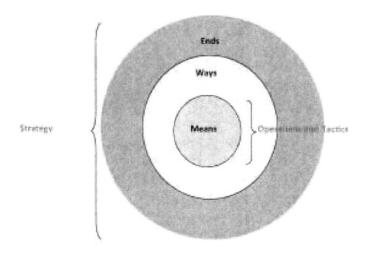

Figure 2. Ends, Ways, and Means in War as a Whole.

In contrast, however, if we conduct a similar analysis with discrete levels of war and their associated levels of command, a hierarchical model emerges such as that in Figure 3.

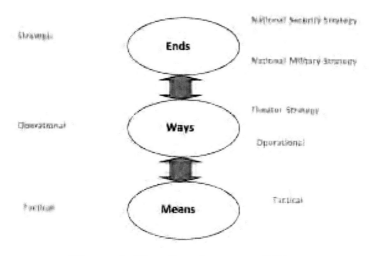

Figure 3. The Continuum of War.

The "Continuum of War" model, accords with most extant western doctrine, reflecting what Eliot Cohen has referred to as the "Huntingtonian" or "normal" theory of civil military relations.[92] In this model, it is the "duty of the statesman to formulate a 'clear, concise, and unambiguous declaration of national policy,' to guide the military that bridged 'the continually irritating gap between the executive and legislature'."[93] Once this was provided, the politicians should simply get out of the way and let the military get on with its job. As was written at the Command and General Staff School in 1936:

> Politics and Strategy are radically and fundamentally things apart. Strategy begins where politics ends. All that soldiers ask is that once the policy is settled, strategy and command shall be regarded as something in a sphere apart from politics. . . . The line of demarcation must be drawn between politics and strategy, supply, and operations. Having found this line, all sides must abstain from trespassing.[94]

Although this is admittedly an extreme view, it continues to echo today. "[A] simplified Huntingtonian concept remains the dominant view within the American defense establishment," with the Caspar Weinberger and Colin Powell doctrines reflecting its continuing authority.[95]

In this vein, Antulio Echevarria has argued that,

> the American way of war tends to shy away from thinking about the complicated process of turning military triumphs, whether on the scale of major campaigns or small-unit actions, into strategic successes. This tendency is symptomatic of a persistent bifurcation in American strategic thinking—though by no means

unique to Americans — in which military professionals concentrate on winning battles and campaigns, while policymakers focus on the diplomatic struggles that precede and influence, or are influenced by, the actual fighting. This bifurcation is partly a matter of preference and partly a by-product of the American tradition of subordinating military command to civilian leadership, which creates two separate spheres of responsibility, one for diplomacy and one for combat. . . . [This means that there is an American way of Battle not an American Way of War]. . . . [T]o move toward a genuine way of war, American military and political leaders must address two key problems. First, they must better define the respective roles and responsibilities of the logic and grammar of war, and, in the process, take steps that will diminish the bifurcation in American strategic thinking. Second, political and military leaders must habituate themselves to thinking more thoroughly about how to turn combat successes into favorable strategic outcomes. Such thinking is not new, but it is clearly not yet a matter of habit. Failure to see the purpose for which a war is fought *as part of war itself* amounts to treating battle as an end in itself.[96]

The existence of an independent level of war served by its own level of command, operating free from unwelcome interference from strategy, represents the foundation on which the U.S. military can define its professional jurisdiction. Performing operational art, as defined in the 1986 version of FM 100-5, represents the pinnacle of the profession of arms. It was therefore both a product of the self-perception of the U.S. military and a necessary input to it. This, arguably, is the true reason for the heretofore unchallenged theoretical solecism that appeared in FM 100-5 in 1982.

Unfortunately, the hierarchical separation of levels of war on which the continuum of war is based is not reflected in practice. Strategy is free to expand, contract, or alter its objectives as circumstances create new opportunities or foreclose others; or as the costs-benefits calculus changes. The connection between war and politics gives strategy its functionality; therefore, war is necessarily vested with the same volatility as politics. Any attempt in theory to insulate the practical conduct of war from this volatility is erroneous. This means that there is not an overlap between strategy, operational art, and tactics, they are completely fused. Tactical actions necessarily carry strategic implications, while strategy conceptualizes, creates, and applies tactical forces, as well as shaping their diplomatic, economic, demographic, and operational environments. An American soldier on a street corner in Baghdad not only personifies a strategic decision to invade Iraq, but also the entire political, social, diplomatic, cultural, and economic evolution of the United States from before its war for independence. The actions of this strategic private are fraught with a broad spectrum of implications—military, Iraqi domestic political, U.S. domestic political, and international political implications. Any attempt to conceptually separate tactics from strategy denies this connection.[97]

The failure to adequately take a truly strategic perspective into campaign planning is manifest in America's recent wars. The 1990-91 Gulf War serves as an example. Yes, in this single campaign, there were two successful instances of operational art: INSTANT THUNDER, the air operation to shape the environment, and DESERT STORM, to eject Iraqi forces from Kuwait. The latter demonstrated many of the characteristics of classical operational art: frontal pressure to suppress the enemy, deep penetration to encircle him, and then a process of attrition of an enemy forced to fight with a reversed front. Both

Heinz Guderian and Tukhachevskiy would have been pleased with DESERT STORM as an operation—a classic *kesselschlacht*. However, despite this success, the 1991 campaign was not sufficient to end the war with Iraq—for which a succession of additional campaigns was required—and which is only now, apparently, coming to a conclusion.

The story of DESERT STORM does not require retelling here. The confusion surrounding the termination of the operation, the negotiation of a cease-fire by General Norman Schwarzkopf in the apparent absence of any guidance from above, and the litany of strategic opportunities thereby foregone, have been comprehensively covered elsewhere. However, they all indicate a surfeit of attention being paid to a single operation and a failure to ensure that the campaign fitted into a strategy. In practice, the operation supplanted the campaign which, in turn, became the strategy. Understandably, Schwarzkopf was focused on the operation—but who was focused on the war?

Iraq (2003-?) is an instructive example of the problems of the existing doctrinal approach. In 2003, who was responsible for anticipating that the campaign to remove Saddam, including another compelling example of Guderian-like operational art, would necessarily be followed by one to establish a successor regime? To simply answer "Bush" or "Rumsfeld" is to hide what has become a doctrinal void. Political leaders are no longer students of war. Therefore, there is a need that their judgment be complemented by wise and candid advisory support to discourage them from demanding the unachievable. Equally though, they need to be made fully aware of the costs and risks attendant on the choices being offered to them. These costs and risks span fields as diverse as minor tactics and international economics, and they are not amenable to adequate consideration at the provincial headquarters of a combatant commander or even in the office of a Secretary of Defense. Binding the conduct of a campaign to that of a war and ensuring the war contributes to the state's role in the march of history is an embodiment of the idea that war is an extension of politics.

The 2007 troop "surge" was conducted when the President, substantially alone, balanced the economic, diplomatic, strategic, political, and military costs and benefits of the alternatives available to him and chose to fight on. This was a return to "classic" campaigning in which the head of state, rather than merely acceding to the advice proferred, laid out the objectives and constraints of the campaign and chose the general who would be responsible.

But the surge aside, disjunctions between politics, strategy, campaign planning, and the conduct of operations were also demonstrated in Somalia (1992) and Kosovo (1998). What allowed the conduct of war and strategy to become so disjointed? How did it come to this? Strategic failure cannot be blamed on any one idea or problem but rather tends, like most accidents, to be the result of a confluence of otherwise unconnected errors. The aim of military doctrine, planning, and organization is to limit the number of errors being made so as to reduce the frequency of these accidents. Not everything is within the control of military leadership, but doctrine largely is. Unsound doctrine is a bad starting point for any war.

The U.S. military's decision to extend the meaning of operational art to encompass campaign planning is a theoretical dead end which perpetuates the failing identified by Echavarria and others. By conflating two very different ideas, the U.S. (and the Anglophone world in lockstep) has reinforced the difficulty of the strategic management of wars and exposed an Achilles heel. At the same time, by expanding the meaning of operational art to be nearly all-encompassing, the detailed examination of its necessary evolution is compromised. When the United States finds itself fighting Serbia, Somali warlords, or failed and failing second and third rank states, these weaknesses may be apparent but their consequences manageable. But if, at some time in the future, the United States finds itself at war with a great power, these theoretical obfuscations may prove to be more damaging.

OPERATIONAL ART: THE NEXT STEPS

> For the enemy the war remained fundamentally . . . a seamless web of political-military-psychological factors to be manipulated by a highly centralized command authority that never took its eye off the political goal of ultimate control of the South. For the United States, however, the war had become by October 1967 a complex of three separate, or only loosely related, struggles: there was a large-scale, conventional war, . . . the confused pacification effort, . . . and the curiously remote air war against North Vietnam.
>
> Townsend Hoopes
> *The Limits of Intervention*

> The great fusion of technologies is impelling the domains of politics, economics, the military, culture, diplomacy, and religion to overlap each other. The connection points are ready, and the trend towards the merging of the various domains is very clear. All of these things are rendering more and more obsolete the idea of confining warfare to the military domain. . . .
>
> Qiao Liang and Wang Xiangsui

71

You fight your war and I'll fight mine.

Mao

A Time After?

This monograph has so far traced the evolution of operational art from its sources in the industrial and political revolutions of the late 18th and early 19th centuries to the present, as well as in the Anglophone world, to the erroneous interpretations dating from the FM 100-5 of 1982 and 1986. The next questions to arise are whether operational art was purely an artifact of the industrial age or whether it has continued relevance as we enter the post-industrial era.

In the successful 1982 British campaign to eject Argentinean forces from the Falklands Islands, the British government, to exploit strong public support for military action before it subsided, directed dispatch of the campaign task force within 3 days of the Argentinean invasion, overriding military advice and forgoing the opportunity for detailed preparation and workup. The Prime Minister, Margaret Thatcher, personally — and in "real time" — approved the sinking of the Argentine cruiser *Belgrano* by HMS *Conqueror*.[98] The Government directed that South Georgia be retaken as soon as possible, despite its military insignificance and in the face of military advice to the contrary, the purpose being to assuage public pressure for action and to sharpen the credibility of British diplomacy. The landings in May 1982 were undertaken despite the failure to achieve air or sea superiority around the Falklands because it was politically unthinkable for the government to consider abandoning operations in the

South Atlantic. There were no indications that a more predominant position could be attained in the short term, and the public's patience was not inexhaustible. Following the landings, and subsequent to the loss from air and missile attack of a number of British ships, the land force commander was directed to engage the enemy at Goose Green despite his argument that it was strategically irrelevant and a distraction. This direction was in response to the enormous public outcry for signs of movement. As Max Hastings and Simon Jenkins put it, "After almost 4 days of unbroken bad news, London needed a tangible victory. If ever there was a politician's battle, then Goose Green was to be it."[99]

Each war is unique, of course, and there is no universally applicable model, but the conduct of the Falklands War demonstrates some characteristics of modern war that need to be accommodated in the further evolution of operational art. From the British perspective, the "ends" of this war went well beyond the liberation of the Falklands. The British decision for war, although taken in justifiable self-defense, was a step in the Thatcherite project to rebuild Britain's self-perception, prestige, and role in the world; therefore, this war was one part of a larger and much more diffuse political competition. The "ways" of the war thus needed to take account both of the specific military problem and of the larger project. Its successful execution demanded continued support from the international community, especially the United States and France, both of whom needed to balance this support with countervailing pressures on them. Accordingly, concern for international perceptions of British actions needed to be balanced against maintenance of British public resolve and a demonstration of British military potency. The Falklands was a truly limited war in which the continuing dialogue among ends, ways, and means required a high degree of political and diplomatic sophistication and the close coupling of tactical action with politics. The Falklands war thus had many of the characteristics of a "modern" war.

In this case, British political leadership was intimately involved in campaign planning and execution. The need to ensure that military action, diplomacy, and public opinion remained in close alignment led the Thatcher government to involve itself quite intimately in the direction of military actions, ranging from the tactical, e.g., to attack Goose Green and sink the *Belgrano*, to the more operational, e.g., to seize South Georgia and accept the risk of proceeding without securing air and sea superiority. The conduct of the war demanded this level of political intervention for strategic "success."[100]

The importance of the intimate involvement of strategy with tactics is futher illuminated by Bob Woodward in *The War Within* (2008), which describes the debates within the U.S. Government surrounding the conduct of the middle stages of the Iraq War.[101] He shows that it was the Bush administration, overcoming the opposition of public opinion, Congress, the Departments of State and Defense, the Joint Chiefs of Staff, and the incumbent commander, which engineered the Surge and framed the subsequent campaign. Without this level of strategic involvement at the highest levels, it would not have been possible to cut through the complex of competing interests to bring the Iraq war to what may now be a satisfactory conclusion.

In the context of this "modern" war, the existing doctrinal orthodoxy that campaign planning and conduct are the privileged province of operational art is demonstrably invalid. If campaign planning and conduct so intimately involve the political level, then the existence of a discrete operational level of war, charged with this responsibility and equipped with its own forms of analysis, is nonsense. If operational art encompasses everything from international politics to the actual preparation for battle, it is so broad an activity as to be doctrinally meaningless.

However, again using the Falklands as an example, the land force efforts to cross the island and seize Port Stanley, and the maritime efforts to establish and enforce exclusion zones around the islands, each represent sequences of tactical actions conducted within a campaign and connected by a unifying idea. In short, then, they meet the 1895 von der Goltz definition of an "operation" and are entirely consonant with Russian and German thinking.[102] As such, they demonstrated operational art—not expressed as a campaign plan here but as a set of connected actions that sought to achieve an objective provided by the campaign plan. It is this traditional relationship between strategy and operations that seems most appropriate to the future of warfare.

Despite continuing debates about the rise or decline of the state, the impacts of resource scarcity, pandemic diseases, urbanization, global warming, economic globalization, demographics, etc., there is a degree of consensus surrounding the likely character of warfare in the next epoch. A number of authors have proposed conceptual models, many of which are worth careful reading. But the one model we find most relevant and interesting here is set forth in the 1999 book by two Chinese People's Liberation Army (PLA) Colonels: Qiao Liang and Wang Xiangsui.[103] *Unrestricted Warfare* was written in the aftermath of the campaigns in Iraq and

Kosovo as a conceptual response to U.S. conventional military predominance. Essentially, it argues for the exploitation and acceleration of a universally accepted trend presently underpinning the evolution of warfare: diffusion.

"Diffusion" describes the blurring of the conceptual boundaries that we have customarily used to aid our understanding and conduct of warfare. The basic premise is that diffusion of warfare from the confines of the traditional battlefield into all the spaces of human activity will inevitably lead to unrestricted warfare:

> The great fusion of technologies is impelling the domains of politics, economics, the military, culture, diplomacy, and religion to overlap each other. The connection points are ready, and the trend towards the merging of the various domains is very clear. All of these things are rendering more and more obsolete the idea of confining warfare to the military domain. . . .[104]

As a result, in unrestricted warfare there is no longer any distinction between what is or is not the battlefield. Spaces in nature, including the ground, the seas, the air, and outer space, are battlefields, but social spaces such as the military, politics, economics, culture, and the psyche are also battlefields. Moreover, the technological space linking these two great spaces is most susceptible of all to serving as a venue for conflict which antagonists spare no effort to win. National power can be military, quasi-military, or nonmilitary. It can employ violence or nonviolence. It can be a confrontation between professional soldiers or between newly emerging forces consisting primarily of ordinary people or experts. These characteristics of unrestricted warfare "mark the watershed between it and traditional warfare, as well as the starting line for new types of warfare."[105]

This theme was taken up and expanded in the Australian Army's concept, *Complex Warfighting*, which noted that the boundaries between war and peace, combatants and noncombatants, the home front and the battlefront, special and conventional operations, state and nonstate actors, military and nonmilitary power, and geographical features themselves, were all in the process of dissolution. Although warfare has always involved the application of all of the instruments of national power and always been intended to impact the psychology of the target population, warfare has customarily expressed these relationships through the application of military force. Diffusion removes the primacy of military force, making it simply one of a suite of levers that can be utilized.

A corollary to the foregoing evolution is that military defeat of the enemy is no longer the principal, or even an important, step on the path to winning a war: annihilation is no longer the objective. The objective of unrestricted war rather is to directly attack the target population's will to resist by attacking its self-perceptions, directly imposing on it the economic and social costs of war, diplomatically isolating it, undermining the morality of its position, and, in short, inducing the people to reject the continuance of the war. It is warfare which focuses on the political aim to the exclusion of all else.[106]

According to its authors, the prosecution of unrestricted war requires:[107]

- **"Omnidirectionality,"** which is "360 degree observation and design involving the combined use of all related factors and making plans . . . employing all measures, and combining the use of all war resources which can be mobilized, to have a field of vision with no blind spots, a concept unhindered by obstacles, and an orientation with no blind angles."

- **"Synchrony,"** which seeks to employ all the military and nonmilitary resources in a concentrated and orchestrated way in temporally compressed wars: "So many objectives which in the past had to be accomplished in stages through an accumulation of battles and campaigns may now be accomplished quickly under conditions of simultaneous occurrence, simultaneous action, and simultaneous completion. Thus, stress on 'synchrony' in combat operations now exceeds the stress on "phasing."

- **"Multidimensional Coordination,"** which refers to coordination and cooperation among different forces in different spheres in order to accomplish an objective. "On the face of it, this definition is not at all novel. . . . The only difference between it and similar explanations is, and this is a great difference, the introduction of nonmilitary and nonwar factors into the sphere of war directly rather than indirectly."

- **"Adjustment and Control of the Entire Process—During the Entire Course of a War, from Its Start, through Its Progress, to its Conclusion, Continually Acquire Information, Adjust Action, and Control the Situation.** Warfare is a dynamic process full of randomness and creativity. Any attempt to tie a war to a set of ideas within a predetermined plan is little short of absurdity or naïveté. Therefore, it is necessary to have feedback and revisions throughout the entire course of a war while it is actually happening to keep the initiative within one's grasp."

The thrust, if not the detail, of *Unrestricted Warfare* represents the current orthodoxy on the ways war will, or should, be fought in the immediate future. The challenges of diffusion and the need to align all the instruments of national power behind the prosecution of war are increasingly represented in the military doctrines of the world. The 2007 U.S. Joint Operating Environment concept is an example. It notes: "Evolving U.S. joint operations doctrine posits a national-level campaign that focuses national capabilities — diplomatic, economic, information, and military — toward averting, deterring, and if necessary winning future conflicts. Once engaged, the United States must consider the political, economic, legal, military, and territorial aspects of the adversary's capability. In complex environments, multiple interactions constantly occur and effects of the specific consequences of military activities will reverberate across each of these domains — and sometimes other unanticipated ones."[108]

In describing the nature of potential U.S. adversaries, the Joint Operating Environment also identifies the weakness in the current U.S. approach to the separation between politics and warfare:

> In their view, American confidence in the technical aspects of war has led to less emphasis on the political foundations of war, in planning for a viable political end state, and in matching national means to this end state. The implications of this foreign perception will be adversaries that are more willing and able to fight in the cultural and political domains. Adversary strategic and operational design will attempt to balance regional requirements to engage or even dominate neighbors, while simultaneously recognizing the need to shaping U.S. perception and engagement, while preparing for conflict with U.S. forces.[109]

The prosecution of our next wars should set the conceptual and doctrinal framework for the further evolution of operational art. Both in its original conception and in its current manifestation, it is suited to strategies of annihilation rather than to those of imposing exhaustion. The delegation of authority and responsibility which underpins our current conceptions of an operational level of war presents lethally dangerous vulnerabilities to a thoughtful enemy.

Unrestricted warfare and the "national campaigns" described in the Joint Operating Environment cannot conceivably be planned or their execution coordinated other than at the highest strategic levels. The interplay of domestic and international politics, diplomacy, economics, and military action executed in both physical space and cyber-space is now so inextricably meshed that political leadership, all of the organs of state bureaucracy, all of the organs of state security, commercial corporations, nongovernmental organizations, as well as fielded military forces need to be aligned and coordinated. The design, planning, and conduct of such a campaign, and the nesting of that campaign in an overall strategy for the conduct of an unrestricted war, together with its ongoing refinement, adjustment, and redirection, is not a job for a joint task force (JTF) commander posted somewhere in the provinces. Now, more than ever, there is a need for true strategic art.

Strategic art involves the continuous orchestration of all the instruments of national power to protect and promote national interests in both war and peace. It therefore involves the perpetual facilitation of the dialogue among ends, ways, and means. It is not a military function, though the military has an essential and unique contribution to make to it. The performance of that function will, however, demand a degree of redefinition of what the profession of arms entails.

Strategic art requires the identification of threats, challenges, and problems; the derivation and articulation of an array of potential measures to counter them; the clustering of these measures in action plans; the attainment of bureaucratic consensus and allocation of resources; and the supervision and subsequent adjustment of implementation. Strategic art is public policy requiring a closing of the customary gap between conception and implementation. As such, we should expect the normal algorithms of public policy to become more dominant. Therefore, rather than a government approaching its military saying, "We've got a war on and we want you to go and beat X," in the era of unrestricted warfare it is just as likely that a military or some other agency will approach its government saying, "We believe we are under attack, and this is our proposed response."

The contribution the military can make in this realm of public policy is a result of its planning culture and bureaucratic focus on the preparation for, and execution of, wars. Military bureaucracies, uniquely in governmental machinery as a rule, see planning as part of a comprehensive effort to address all existing and potential problems, not solely a response to immediate problems. Viewed from the civilian world, military planning is essentially a comprehensive risk management method in which the consequences of the occurrence of events at risk is "disaster." Because they provide the venue for the confluence of intelligence, a national security focus, long-service national security professionals, and a planning culture, military bureaucracies are arguably the only organizations able to identify and coordinate a response to the multi-modal, hard-to-recognize, and hard-to-define threats typical of unrestricted warfare. The obligation therefore rests on them to accept the responsibility to exercise bureaucratic leadership so as to stimulate and organize national responses to diffuse, often nonmilitary, threats. This necessarily involves campaign planning as a bureaucracy-centric rather than commander-centric activity, and therefore rests on influence and peer leadership more than it does on command authority or direction. Only military bureaucracies at the seat of government can exercise strategic art to plan and execute "national campaigns" of the sort envisaged, for example, in the Joint Operating Environment.

Campaign planning should be a strategic artifact, conducted in national capitals and involving the detailed coordination of domestic and international politics with military, diplomatic, economic, and informational actions. This resulting multi-modal campaign will likely comprise a number of lines of operation, both military and nonmilitary. Within this multi-modal campaign, there are two alternative models for operational art:

- It can be focused on the achievement of the campaign objectives within one line of operation, either within a geographic subdivision of the theater, or within the theater as a whole; or,
- It can be focused on the achievement of campaign objectives for all the lines of operation within a geographic subdivision of the theater.

It is clear from the doctrines of the Anglophone armies that we aspire to the latter model in which the relevant commander is applying both military and nonmilitary resources to the achievement of objectives in social, political, economic, and security arenas within his assigned boundaries. The extent to which this more attractive comprehensive model is achievable will depend on the extent to which strategic art is able to establish unity of command. It is only sensible to ask a commander to conduct multi-modal operations across a number of lines of operation if he is also delegated control over the necessary resources. The procedures for this in the military are well established, but control of interagency and other resources remains problematic.

Without this control, the independence necessary for the commander to sequence tactical actions in pursuit of campaign objectives — i.e., to perform operational art — is missing. Resolving conflicting interagency priorities, work practices, and worldviews by negotiation and consensus-building may be necessary in today's complex operations, but it is not operational art: it is simply muddling through. The type of multi-modal coordination described, for example, in the Australian Army's concept *Adaptive Campaigning, the U.S. Joint Operating Environment,* and the British *Comprehensive Approach* cannot be realized without the establishment of a high degree of unity of command across military and nonmilitary agencies that is, in turn, further delegated to geographically focused headquarters.[110] This is a worthy aspiration, but one which will likely remain only aspiration until demands arise that are more compelling than the current rash of small wars.

Even the less ambitious first model above is exceedingly difficult, but it at least proffers the prospect of practicality. In this model, military or nonmilitary leaders would be responsible for sequencing actions within a specified line of operation. This allows the problems of interagency coordination, at least potentially, to be managed as part of the management of the campaign as a whole instead of becoming a problem delegated to some hapless junior commander. If strategic art is able to achieve sufficient bureaucratic consensus to deliver a practical level of unity of command within a line of operation, then there may be opportunities to achieve operational art within that line.

This, however, again threatens to take a relatively simple idea and extend it into new and untested areas. Are actions sequenced within a line of operation focused on infrastructure or law and order actually operational art? They fit the formal definition but may no longer involve military resources, military objectives, or military command. Is extending its meaning into this realm productive or useful? In answering this question, we must go to the functions of any military theory. Does "it" (the redefinition) help us better understand the problem of war, train individuals, structure organizations, or acquire equipment? Does it explain the military problem to political leadership? Again, it seems to us that by unwittingly extending the meaning of operational art to meet emerging conceptual needs, its meaning and military utility are diluted and devalued. Interagency cooperation needs be explained, trained, and done by governments, it needs be taught to commanders, and the military needs to be prepared to participate. This does not, however, define its place in theory. Interagency coordination within a campaign is not necessarily operational art because not everything that happens within a campaign is.

If operational art were to be returned to its traditional enclosure—as the sequencing of tactical actions to achieve objectives provided by the campaign plan — and if it were to retain its traditional focus on the enemy, then it has utility as an intellectual framework supporting the preparation for war. It would not, however, be the war but simply an aspect of warfare to be exploited or ignored as the circumstances demand.

In acknowledging the complexity and interconnectedness of contemporary conflict, there is a tendency to be apologetic about the use of force — as if it is in some sense a measure of failure. Very likely, this is principally a result of our present overconcentration on counterinsurgency. In any event, we need to be careful lest it overwhelm the core of the profession of arms — which is the skillful use of those arms. Tactical combat remains the basis of all military endeavor. The challenges of choosing who, when, where, and how to fight to achieve an assigned mission remain the most important ones facing soldiers. Traditional operational art helps meet those challenges. The selection of objectives to which operational art should strive, and their relationship with actions in other lines of operation, remain a problem for campaign planning and conduct which is, at least for the present, beyond the purview or capacity of operational art to resolve.

CONCLUSION: OPERATIONAL ART IS NOT THE WHOLE OF WARFARE — ONLY A DISCRETIONARY PART OF IT

> Strategical and tactical matters often flow into each other.
>
> Von der Goltz, 1895

> The kind of thinking we have called "operational art" is often now required at battalion level.
>
> Wass de Czega, 2009

It is in the nature of revolutions that they destroy what they replace. The 1982 introduction of the operational level of war into the Anglophone lexicon was, in this sense, truly revolutionary: it can be said to have destroyed strategy as it was. This monograph has dwelt on the historical and elemental roots of the theoretical and practical underpinnings of the terms "operational art" and "levels of war," and explained the consequences for strategy. That analysis provides context for a discussion of the need to revisit doctrine and perhaps pause before piling new conceptual theory—currently systems and systems design—on a flawed idea. In the remainder of this monograph, we initiate that discussion, revisiting our key themes in the process.

There was a time when the world had no need for operational art: a time when sovereigns led their armies in the field and where the yoking of war to politics was his or her personal undertaking. It was the sovereigns who chose whether or not to fight, where to fight, and for how long to fight, and it was they who were constantly balancing opportunities and threats, risks and returns, costs and benefits. In the era of "strategies of a single point," the connections between tactics and statecraft were immediate and intimate.

As modern states emerged, their economic and social organization enabled them to deploy and sustain armies of ever expanding size. The nation fielding such armies was increasingly linked to their sustainment and to their success or failure. This meant that the conduct of operations was increasingly geared to the capacity and willingness of the citizens to pay the price of victory in both blood and treasure. The Army became, more than ever, an extension of the will of the state, that was, itself, an extension of the will of the people. Louis XIV's dictum *"L'etat, c'est moi"* became *"l'etat, c'est nous."* Accordingly, national leaders were required not just to manage the international politics of war but domestic politics at war. This meant that the "logic" that supported the selection of a course of action was decreasingly likely to be purely, or even predominantly, military.

General Ulysses Grant's campaign in Northern Virginia in 1864 is an excellent example of the power of this new domestic political influence. Having appointed Grant as General in Chief in March of that election year, President Abraham Lincoln's direction to him was to take Richmond.[111] In addition to this injunction, because he feared the adverse electoral impact of yet another Confederate raid on Washington, Lincoln insisted that Grant keep the Army of the Potomac squarely between that city and General Robert E. Lee's Army of Virginia. This obliged Grant to campaign overland through northern Virginia rather than exploit the Atlantic flank by approaching Richmond through North Carolina. Lincoln also ordered Grant to appoint Generals Benjamin Butler and Franz Sigel to command two supporting offensives on the James River and in the Shenandoah Valley, respectively.[112] Butler was a prominent Democrat with presidential aspirations, and Lincoln was keen to show that he was not fighting a solely Republican war. Sigel, on the other hand, brought with him a large constituency of German immigrants. Both Butler and Sigel failed, and Grant, after The Wilderness, Spotsylvania Courthouse, and Cold Harbor, eventually found himself southeast of Richmond — probably not too far from where he would have started without Lincoln's directives.

The intimacy of the relationship between politics and the conduct of war is also apparent in subsesquent events. By 1864, the Confederacy was economically broken and scraping the bottom of its pool of manpower, whereas the Union was growing in both economic and military power. However, if the northern electorate had rejected Lincoln in the election of 1864, there was every possibility of the Confederacy achieving a negotiated peace based on the overturning of the Emancipation Proclamation and, in effect, a return to the *status quo ante*. In terms of the Union war effort, the cost in blood of the campaign in northern Virgina, the extension of the war into 1865, General Jubal Early's raid on Washington in July resulting from Sigel's failure, and Butler's failure on the James River could all be recovered from. But a defeat by Lincoln in the election could not have been recouped.

In addition to this tightening of the coupling between national politics and the conduct of operations, the expansion of war also had two important consequences for the evolution of operational art: the need for a succession of blows to defeat a modern nation-state and the problem of linking tactical actions across an ever expanding theater of operations to the political purposes of the war.

Wars are fought to redistribute political power across national boundaries. The most worn path to that redistribution has been for each of the belligerents to attempt to remove the powers of resistance of the other. In the era of strategies of a single point, this was often, at least notionally, accomplished in a single climactic battle. As armies grew, however, and as the size of the theater of operations grew accordingly, the prospects of defeating the armed forces of a modern state in a single decisive battle receded dramatically. As a result, the need for a number of battles to be connected in such a way as to most effectively and economically disarm the enemy was widely recognized. In Europe at least, warfare was typically based on the annihilation of the armed forces of the enemy and typically required the connection of a number of battles.

The expansion of the theater of operations also removed the actions of those armies from the direct scrutiny of the sovereign, with the connection between war and politics becoming unacceptably stretched. In an era of poor communications, the problems of coordinating the actions of armies that might be spread across the continent of Europe became increasingly salient. If the sovereign could not be present to link tactics with politics, how could he be confident that this connection was in some way being made?

The idea of the campaign was expanded to fill the dual need: the need to connect a succession of battles to disarm the enemy, and the need to reconnect tactics and politics. To do this, the term "campaign" gained a geographic meaning in addition to its traditional temporal one. The campaign had always been a discrete and identifiable portion of the war which somehow contributed to the favorable resolution of the whole, but it grew to mean not only a set of activities within a temporally circumscribed "season" but became, as necessary, the pursuit of the war's objectives by an independent commander acting beyond the immediate scrutiny of his sovereign. The objectives which this commander strove to achieve, however, were not his own; rather, they were laid down by the sovereign and formed the bridge between the specific campaign and the wider war.

The framework provided by the direction, campaign objectives, geographic boundaries, resources, and other necessaries provided by the sovereign determined the freedom of action available to the campaign commander. Within those freedoms, he was able to sequence battles as he thought necessary so as to achieve the objectives that had been assigned to him. The entirety of the campaign objectives might, on occasion, be achieved by a single sequence of battles. More likely, however, a number of sequences, each directed at somehow setting the conditions for the next step, would be necessary. In the former case, the "**operation**" or **sequence of tactical actions connected by a unifying idea,** and the "campaign" were synonymous. In the latter case, the campaign consisted of a number of separate operations that each contributed to the whole. The cascading hierarchy of objectives—political, strategic, campaign, operational, and tactical—reconnected tactical action to the political purposes of the war and again, at least notionally, enabled the succession of blows delivered by an independent commander to contribute directly to the annihilation of the enemy army as a whole.

World War I was the quintessential European dynastic war. Although the objective technological, economic, and social conditions that determined the character of warfare were quite familiar in the West, the failure of the initial plans of the Germans and French led to the establishment of a stabilized front with no apparently assailable flank. Along this front, the tactical defensive power conferred by the combination of field fortifications, artillery, and machine guns, in combination with the ability conferred by railways to move masses of men and materiel from place to place along it, created a military problem to which no solution was found during the course of the war.

In the period after World War I, while the world's political leaders were busy redistributing political power and creating the League of Nations, soldiers got on with preparing for the next war. The military problems that World War I had presented became the focus of that preparation. In Germany, they resulted in tactical innovations intended to restore effective striking power to the tactical offensive — *Blitzkrieg* — which would reenable the preferred forms for German large-scale maneuver — *kesselschlacht* – intended to annihilate the armed forces of the enemy.

In the USSR similar responses to the challenges highlighted by World War I led to the identification of operational art as a discrete component of military science. After a lengthy debate, the Soviets settled on the **deep attack** as the basic offensive technique. This involved a general offensive to suppress the enemy's ability to conduct defensive maneuver, the application of enormously powerful combined arms armies to create penetrations, and then the extension of these penetrations into the depth of the enemy defensive layout to encircle large agglomerations of combat power preparatory to their annihilation.

It was within the context of the extension of the initial penetrations that the role for operational art first emerged. To maintain momentum and continue to deepen the penetrations faster than the enemy could respond, deep echelonment of forces was envisaged. As each echelon achieved its objectives, its successor would assume the lead and push on to its own objectives, etc. Within each of these echelons, typically at the level of army command, there would be a succession of battles by regiments, by divisions, or by the army as a whole intended to both secure the objective and annihilate the enemy forces occupying the geographic space between the starting point and the objective. This formed the operation, decisive within its own depth, and within which lay the opportunity for the application of operational art in the thoughtful combination of tactics and logistics to meet the objectives of the operation.

Good operational art made for successful operations, successful operations contributed to a successful deep attack, successful deep attacks led to the encirclement of the enemy, and the continuation of the general offensive that had initially suppressed the enemy front led to the annihilation of the encircled enemy. Repetition of this mechanism would eventually lead to the disarming of the enemy and the opportunity for the USSR to dictate the terms of the subsequent peace. "Operations" and operational art in the USSR were essential but modest components of military science, clearly subordinate to the campaign plan which was itself a product of the supreme headquarters working in conjunction with the political leadership in the European strategic context.

The Anglophone world remained throughout this revolution largely oblivious to the emergence of the operation or the advent of operational art and arguably a relatively smaller body of formal land doctrine addressing issues above tactical training. Attitudes in the West began to change with the rise of NATO and saw marked movement in 1982 when the U.S. Army published FM-100-5, reintroducing to English the idea of "operations," and in the 1986 version, the term "operational art." During this same period, probably for a combination of reasons, rather than adopting the prevailing understanding of the meanings and role of operations and operational art, the U.S. Army acceded to the idea of an operational level of war and introduced it to NATO. Our research has established that this new "level" was simply an artifact. While giving "nodding acknowledgment" to the German and Soviet theorists, it had no historical or practical precursors and represented at best a convenient analytical way station for training purposes. Unfortunately, it also established a point of departure for a new and profoundly erroneous interpolation in military theory.

In the American/NATO usage of FM-100-5, rather than meeting its original purpose of contributing to the attainment of campaign objectives laid down by strategy, operational art—practiced as a "level of war"—assumed the responsibility for campaign planning and, by reducing the political leadership to the role of "strategic sponsors," quite specifically widened the gap between politics and warfare. The result has been a well-demonstrated ability to win battles that have not always contributed to strategic success, i.e., "a way of battle rather than a way of war." To a large extent, the creation of an operational level of war undid all the good effort to constructively connect politics and tactics that had been expended by theorists since Moltke.

This pernicious solecism—operational level of war—has confused our response to the continuing evolution of warfare. At a time when the connections between tactics and politics are being continuously strengthened and exploited by actual and putative enemies, we have stretched the meaning of operational art until it has become a near synonym for the entirety of warfare. In combination with its role as a defining component of the jurisdiction of the profession of arms, it has effectively discouraged us from making the institutional adaptations necessary to cope with the increasing connectedness of the more-military and less-military aspects of contemporary warfare.

Clausewitz's dictum that war is an extension of politics by other means is universally recognized and lauded—but perhaps not always understood in practice. To be fully understood it might have to be paired with former Speaker of the House Tip O'Neill's aphorism that "all politics is local." Strategists and soldiers tend to see war as an extension of *policy*— the pursuit of rationally derived goals through the application of effort commensurate with their professional responsibility. Clausewitz, arguably demonstrating greater wisdom, saw war as an extension of *politics*—"a chaotic process involving competing personalities (whose *individual* actions may indeed have a rational basis), chance and friction, and popular emotion."[113] In a war, the actions of all of the protagonists are determined by this interaction of policy and politics. To isolate one from the other is to ignore a critical part of the whole.

The political leadership of a country cannot simply set objectives for a war, provide the requisite materiel, then stand back and await victory. Nor should the nation or its military be seduced by this prospect. Politicians must necessarily be concerned with the minute-to-minute conduct of war and today's plethora of military actions. Only thus can they adjust to the working of the adversary's remarkable trinity and that of other interested states, while managing their own "trinity." Thus political considerations are "influential in the planning of war, of the campaign, and often even of the battle."[114] Clausewitz further cautions us that multiple points of view—administrative, military, political—cannot be a basis for planning wars and that the political perspective must be given precedence over everything.[115]

Faced with U.S. military strength as the backbone of military power in "The West," thoughtful enemies will seek paths to victory that do not rest solely on direct military contests with the United States. The Vietnam War demonstrated to the world the fractiousness of U.S. politics. Though the North Vietnamese were seemingly accidental beneficiaries of it, their experience has provided a lesson widely recognized by putative adversaries. There is in Liang and Xiangsui's *Unrestricted War* and other present literature a recognition that American confidence in the technological aspects of war has traditionally led to less emphasis on its political foundations, leading to a popular reluctance to keep the nation's shoulder to the wheel. The result of this broad perception will be adversaries that seek to fight us more in the cultural and political domains than in the military. Such enemies do not buy into neat mechanistic warfare based on the defense of bureaucratic jurisdictions. Rather, they require that all of the instruments of national power be considered as fingers on the right hand of government.

If operational art is the entirety of warfare from campaign design down to battalion level—and if it is principally the purview of the military—then the type of "national campaigns" envisaged in the Joint Operating Environment, seeking the coherent and direct application of all of the instruments of national power, are beyond our reach. Perhaps we should use the term "strategic art" to encompass the bureaucratic effort required to deal with the types of diffuse, nuanced, and complex problems we anticipate in the future. At present, operational art is filling that space—as it unthinkingly threatens to fill the space occupied by tactics and even minor tactics: if battalion commanders are operational artists, as suggested in the quotation at the start of this section, then surely the strategic corporal also needs to be one.

Despite the doctrine presently published by the world's militaries, doctrine which preaches independence for combatant commanders, there is no evidence that politicians are content to set concrete objectives and then sit back and passively watch the conduct of a war for which they are responsible to both their domestic and international constituencies now and for the rest of history. The development of a military theory based on a rejection of empirical experience in favor of an undemonstrated ideal does not guarantee failure — but it makes failure more likely. The U.S. theory of an operational level of war charged with campaign planning and working in conjunction with the existing post-Goldwater-Nichols security hierarchy threatens effective campaign planning. Specifically, it threatens to resist close engagement with the political and bureaucratic leadership until strategic pressures become intolerable, at which time the "10,000-mile screw driver" pierces the carapace of the operational commander, often to his chargrin. Or, more usually, the operational level theory means that a campaign is undertaken without the strategic level being fully engaged in examination of the ends-ways-means interaction, with resulting self-imposed strategic surprise which needs to be dealt with as the war progresses.

The result has been characterized as "compression" of the operational level of war, in which the strategic level is charged with being guilty of intrusion into the realms of operations and tactics. If the reader accepts the journey of discovery embodied in this monograph, he or she will reject the foregoing charge. Operational art arose as the industrial revolution expanded the battlefield with the result that strategy was unable to sustain adequate intimacy in its dialogue with tactics. The more limited character of contemporary wars and the state of communications technologies have now removed these barriers, making it feasible for strategy to reconnect with tactics in the way nature intended. Rather than the operational level being compressed, strategy is reasserting its rightful role and attempting to meet its responsibilities, this in the face of the dual resistances presented by the enemy and a dysfunctional military doctrine.

The term "operational art" can mean anything we decree it to mean, but it cannot usefully mean everything we presently think it does. It is not at all clear that interagency operational art is practical nor that a logical line of operation seeking to establish the rule of law in a vanquished foe can truly be said to contain opportunities for operational art. Arguably, we are confusing the terms "operational art" and "purposeful action." To be useful, trainable, and applicable, operational art must have meaningful boundaries.

As the West becomes increasingly apologetic about the application of force, the original meaning and purpose of operational art—the thoughtful combination of tactics and logistics to achieve assigned objectives (principally the annihilation of the enemy)—has become hidden by the well-intentioned but problematic attempt to "do good," rather than simply stopping the enemy from "doing bad." Even in today's counterinsurgencies, the sequences of tactical actions necessary to destroy the enemy's military capabilities and capacity present generous scope for the application of operational art as it was originally conceived. However, as long as we confuse operational art with the distribution of electricity to the civilian populace, we are unlikely to find the clarity necessary to do this.

It is time we returned operational art to its original province. Without good strategy which acknowledges the abstractions and dynamism of politics and designs campaigns accordingly, operational art is bereft of its guiding logic and becomes pointless. Operational art is not the entirety of warfare. Operational art is not the design and conduct of campaigns. Operational art is not an interagency problem. Operational art is the thoughtful sequencing of tactical actions to defeat a component of the armed forces of the enemy. Good operational art, demonstrated as often as necessary to support the achievement of campaign objectives, ensures that tactical actions contribute to the attainment of the purpose of a war — and that is all.

BIBLIOGRAPHY

Australian Army. *Adaptive Campaigning*, Army Headquarters, Canberra ACT, 2008.

_____. *Complex Warfighting*, Army Headquarters, Canberra ACT 2003.

Australian Defense Force, *ADDP-D Doctrine I*, Army Headquarters, Canberra ACT 2002.

Beyerchen, Alan D. "Clausewitz Non-linearity and the Unpredictability of War," *International Security*, 17:3, Winter 1992.

Boot, M. *The Savage Wars of Peace: Small Wars and the Rise of American Power*, New York: Basic Books, 2002.

Brand, Dieter. "The Origins of *Freie Operationen*," *Military Review*, Fort Leavenworth, KS, July/August 2000.

British Ministry of Defence. *British Defence Doctrine, JDPO-01*, 2008.

_____. *Joint Doctrine Note 4/05, The Comprehensive Approach*, Shrivenham, Wilts: British Ministry of Defence, 2002.

Bucholz, Arden. *Moltke, Schlieffen, and Prussian War Planning*, Oxford, UK: Berg Publishers, 1991.

Clark, A. *Barbarossa*, London, UK: Cassell, 2005.

Clausewitz, Carl von. *On War*, Michael Howard and Peter Paret, eds., Princeton, NJ: Princeton University Press, 1984.

Cohen, Eliot. *Supreme Command: Soldiers, Statesmen, and Leadership in Wartime*, New York: Free Press. 2002.

Cooper, Matthew. *The German Army 1933-45: Its Political and Military Failure*, London, UK: Macdonald and Janes, 1978, p. 133.

Corum, J. S. *The Roots of Blitzkrieg*, Lawrence: University of Kansas Press, 1992.

Craig, Gordon A. *The Battle of Koniggratz*, Philadelphia, PA, and New York: J. B. Lippincot Co., 1964.

Doughty, Robert A. *The Breaking Point: Sedan and the Fall of France, 1940*, Hamden, CT: Archon, 1990.

Echevarria, A. J. *After Clausewitz: German Military Thinkers Before the Great War*, Lawrence: University of Kansas Press, 2000.

_____. *Towards An American Way of War*, Carlisle, PA: Strategic Studies Institute, U.S. Army War College, March 2004.

Foote, Shelby. "Another Grand Design," *The Civil War, A Narrative*, Vol. VII, New York: Random House, 1974.

Evans, Michael. "From Kadesh to Kandahar: Military Theory and the Future of War," *Naval War College Review*, Summer 2003.

Gat, Azar. *A History of Military Thought*, Oxford, UK: Oxford University Press, 2001.

_____. "Liddell-Hart's Theory of Armoured Warfare: Revising the Revisionists," *The Journal of Strategic Studies*, Vol. 19, No. 1, March 1996.

Glantz, David M. "Soviet Operational Art Since 1936: The Triumph of Maneuver War," Bruce W. Menning (ed.), *Historical Perspectives of the Operational Art*, Carlisle, PA: Military History Institute.

Goerlitz, Walter. *The German General Staff*, New York: Praeger, 1953.

Grimsley, Mark. "Surviving Military Revolution: The U.S. Civil War," MacGregor Knox and Williamson Murray (eds.), *The Dynamics of Military Revolution 1300-2050*, Cambridge, MA: Cambridge University Press, 2001.

Guderian, H. *Panzer Leader*, London, UK: Futura Publications, 1976.

Handel, Michael. *Masters of War: Classical Strategic Thought*, London, UK: Cass, 2001.

Hastings, Max, and Simon Jenkins, *The Battle for the Falklands*, London, UK: Michael Joseph, 1983.

Henderson, G. F. R. "Strategy and its Teaching," *Journal of the RUSI*, No. 42, July 1898.

Hoffman, Frank. *Hybrid Wars*, Arlington, VA: Potomac Institute for Policy Studies, 2007.

Hughes, Daniel J. *Moltke on the Art of War*, Novato, CA: Presidio Press, 1993.

Isserson, G. "Operational Prospects for the Future," H. S. Orenstein, ed., *The Evolution of Soviet Operational Art: The Documentary Basis*, Portland, OR: Frank Cass, 1995.

_____. "The Evolution of Operational Art," H. S. Orenstein, ed., *The Evolution of Soviet Operational Art: The Documentary Basis*, Portland, OR: Frank Cass, 1995.

Jomini, Antoine Henri. "Summary of the Art of War," *Roots of Strategy Book 2*, Harrisburg, PA: Stackpole Books, 1987.

Keegan, John. *Mask of Command*, London, UK: Pimlico, 2004.

Liddell-Hart, B. H. *Strategy*, New York: Meridian, 1991.

_____. *Sherman*, London, UK: Dodd, Mead and Co., 1929.

Lykke, A. F. "Toward an Understanding of Military Strategy," *Military Review*, May 1989.

Manstein, Erich von. *Lost Victories*, London, UK: Greenhill Books, Herts, 1987.

Mariyevsky, I. "Formation and Development of the Theory of Operational art (1918-38)," H. S. Orenstein, ed., *The Evolution of Soviet Operational Art, 1927-1964: The Documentary Basis,* London, UK: Frank Cass, 1995.

Matheny, Michael R. *In the Beginning,* unreferenced photocopy passed to the authors by Colonel Matheny in 2001.

McKerchner, B. J., and M. C. Hennessy, eds. *The Operational Art: Developments in the Theory of War,* Westport, CT: Praeger, 1996.

Naveh, Shimon. *In Pursuit of Military Excellence: The Evolution of Operational Theory.* Portland, OR: Frank Cass, 1997.

Orenstein, H. S. *The Evolution of Soviet Operational Art: The Documentary Basis,* Portland, OR: Frank Cass, 1995.

Osgood, Robert E. *Limited War: The Challenge to American Strategy,* Chicago, IL: University of Chicago Press, 1957.

Qiao Liang and Wang Xiangsui. *Unrestricted Warfare,* Beijing, China: People's Liberation Army Literature and Arts Publishing House, February 1999.

Reid, Brian Holden. *Studies in British Military Thought – Debates with Fuller and Liddell-Hart,* Lincoln: University of Nebraska Press, 1998.

Rosinski, Herbert. "Scharnhorst to Schlieffen: "The Rise and Decline of German Military Thought," *Naval War College Review,* Summer 1976.

Schneider, James J. *The Structure of a Strategic Revolution,* Novato CA: Presidio Press, 1994.

Simpkin, R. E. *Deep Battle, The Brainchild of Marshal Tukhachevsky,* London, UK: Brassey's Defense Publishers, 1987.

Starry, General Donn A. "A Perspective on American Military Thought," *Military Review,* July 1989.

Svechin, A. A. *Strategy and Operational Art*, H. S. Orenstein, ed., *The Evolution of Soviet Operational Art: The Documentary Basis*, Portland, OR: Frank Cass, 1995.

Tuchman, Barbara. *The Guns of August*, New York: Macmillan Publishing Company, 1988.

Tukhachevsky, M. "Voyna klopov," *Revolyustiya I voyna*, No. 22, 1923. As quoted in Jacob Kipp, "Two Views of Warsaw: The Russian Civil War and Soviet Operational Art, 1920-1932," B. J. McKerchner and M. C. Hennessy, eds., *The Operational Art: Developments in the Theory of War*, Westport, CT: Praeger, 1996.

U.S. Department of the Army. *The German Campaign in Russia: Planning and Operations (1940-42)*, Washington, DC, 1955.

U.S. Joint Forces Command. *Joint Operating Environment: Trends and Challenges for the Future Joint Operating Force through 2030*, Norfolk, VA, 2007.

Villacres, E. J., and C. Bassford. "Reclaiming the Remarkable Trinity," *Parameters*, Autumn 1995.

Von der Goltz, Baron Colmar. "The Operations," Section 8, *The Conduct of War*, 1895. A photocopy of which, produced by the U.S. Army War College Art of War Colloquium in February 1983, is in the possession of the author.

Wallach, J. L. *The Dogma of the Battle of Annihilation: The Theories of Clausewitz and Schlieffen and Their Impact on the German Conduct of Two World Wars*, Westport, CT: Greenwood Press, 1986.

Wass de Czega, Huba. "Systemic Operational Design: Learning and Adapting In Complex Missions," *Military Review*, January/February 2009.

Woodward, Bob. *The War Within: A Secret White House History*, New York: Simon and Schuster, 2008.

Ziemke, E. F. "The Soviet Theory of Deep Operations," *Parameters*, Vol. XIII, No. 2, 1982.

ENDNOTES

1. Shimon Naveh, *In Pursuit of Military Excellence: The Evolution of Operational Theory*, Portland, OR: Frank Cass, 1997, p. 186.

2. This is an esoteric point that might require enlargement. The extreme case is instructive because the linkages are clear. The act of employing a nuclear weapon is tactical—but the strategic consequences extend not just to the resolution of the specific war but also to the world order that prevails afterwards and the relative standing of the countries using or impacted by the weapons. The same problem is attendant on the use of all weapons although not in as overt or extreme a manner. The debate about the Israeli use of cluster bombs in Lebanon in 2006 and of white phosphorus in Gaza in 2008-09 present examples of this connection between the tactical and strategic.

3. Herbert Rosinski, "Scharnhorst to Schlieffen: 'The Rise and Decline of German Military Thought'," *Naval War College Review*, Summer 1976, p. 85.

4. *Ibid.*, p. 103.

5. Michael I. Handel, *Masters of War: Classical Strategic Thought*, London, United Kingdom: Frank Cass, 2001, p. 345.

6. Huba Wass de Czega, "Systemic Operational Design: Learning and Adapting in Complex Missions," *Military Review*, January/February 2009. We think that, in the language of Isaiah Berlin, this makes Sun Tsu and Confucius foxes, and we in the West hedgehogs:

> [F]oxes seek many ends at the same time and see the world in all its complexity, [but] never integrating their thinking into one overall concept. Hedgehogs simplify a complex world into a single, organizing idea, a basic principle that organizes and guides everything. A hedgehog reduces all challenges and dilemmas to simple—indeed almost simplistic—hedgehog ideas. Hedgehogs understand that the essence of profound insight is simplicity. Hedgehogs aren't simpletons: they

have a piercing insight that allows them to see through complexity and discern underlying patterns.

Perhaps there is still a debate to be had about the relative advantages that foxes and hedgehogs might bring to today's "complex missions."

7. Here, for the students of systems theory, it is important to recognize that the belligerent systems do not "compete" in the systems sense, within a shared rule set. Rather, they are in combat, each intent on the subversion of the other's "ends," to the advantage of their own. In a formal sense, one end state/steady state cannot be designed without the participation of, rather than merely intimate knowledge of, the other. In combat this occurs at the peace, not before.

8. In the Franco-Prussian War of 1870-71, for example, King of Prussia Frederick Wilhelm; his Chancellor, Bismarck; and the Chief of the General Staff, Moltke, all shared a single deployed headquarters, whereas on the French side, Napoleon III and substantial portions of his cabinet were similarly deployed.

9. Antoine Henri Jomini, "Summary of the Art of War," *Roots of Strategy Book 2*, Harrisburg, PA: Stackpole Books, 1987, p. 460. Colonel G. F. R. Henderson took up this idea and explained that grand tactics were to minor tactics what the latter were to drill. They involve adapting the power of combination to the requirements of battle. More intriguingly, Henderson notes that Grand Tactics "deal principally with moral factors"; and their chief end is the concentration of superior force, moral and physical, at the decisive point and are "the art of generalship [and] include those stratagems, maneuvers, and devices by which victories are won, and concern only those officers who may find themselves in independent command." This is more expansive than Jomini and begins to create a bridge to what we would today call operational art. G. F. R. Henderson, "Strategy and its Teaching," *Journal of the RUSI*, No. 42, July 1898, p. 767.

10. He notes:

Grand Tactics is the art of forming good combinations preliminary to battles as well as during their progress.

The guiding principle in tactical combinations, as in those of strategy, is to bring the mass of the force at hand against a part of the opposing army and upon that point the possession of which promises the most important results. . . . I am of the opinion that if it be a general's design to make himself master of his enemy's communications while at the same time holding his own, he should employ strategic rather than tactical combinations.

Jomini, pp. 494-495.

11. *Ibid.*, p. 461.

12. *Ibid.*, p. 439.

13. *Ibid.*, p. 447.

14. See Handel, pp. 435-452, which discusses Clausewitz' *Gestalt* view of war; and Alan D. Beyerchen, "Clausewitz Nonlinearity and the Unpredictability of War," *International Security*, Vol. 17, No. 3, Winter, 1992, pp. 55-90.

15. For an expansion on this argument, see E. J. Villacres and C. Bassford, "Reclaiming the Remarkable Trinity," *Parameters*, Carlisle, PA: U.S. Army War College, Autumn 1995.

16. Carl von Clausewitz, *On War*, M. Howard and P. Paret, eds., Princeton, NJ: Princeton University Press, 1984, book 2, chap. 1.

17. Daniel J. Hughes, *Moltke on the Art of War*, Novato, CA: Presidio Press, 1993. Many of Moltke's writings on war include much that is either directly quoted from, or which rests heavily on, Clausewitz.

18. Gordon A. Craig, *The Battle of Koniggratz*, Philadelphia, PA, and New York: J B Lippincot Co., 1964, p. xi.

19. *Ibid.*, p. 175.

20. The literature is rich with discussion of Schlieffen's approach to operational art and its consequences for the conduct

of World War I, for example, but in reality Schlieffen and the German General Staff were conducting strategic art by linking the processes of war initiation, mobilization, and deployment to set the conditions for the start of a number of simultaneous campaigns that were connected by a unifying strategic idea.

21. We think that an argument could be made that operational art was actually born during the American Civil War where in the campaign in the West, General William T. Sherman sequenced tactical action in accordance with a campaign design provided by General Ulysses Grant. For whatever reasons, however, this did not influence the development of theory and so represents an early but terminal branch on the evolution of the theory of operational art which took place exclusively in Europe until well after World War II.

22. G. Isserson, "The Evolution of Operational art," H. S. Orenstein, ed., *The Evolution of Soviet Operational art: 1927-1991: The Documentary Basis*, London, UK: Frank Cass, 1995, p. 55.

23. Although Königgrätz was preceded by three subordinate battles, Gitchin, Tratenau, and Nachod, they were all part of a concentric movement of forces towards the focus of Königgrätz. In contrast, the war of 1870 opened with the battles of Werth and Spicheren which were fought as elements of an expanding front.

24. Isserson, "The Evolution," p. 59.

25. A. J. Echevarria, *After Clausewitz: German Military Thinkers Before the Great War*, Lawrence: University of Kansas Press, 2000, p. 212. In 1905 Schlieffen, Chief of the German General Staff, recognized the importance of the overall battle when he invoked it as a means of overcoming the trend for contemporary operations to slip into positional warfare, as had occurred in the Russo-Japanese War. He therefore demanded unceasing combat activity all along the line with all engagements, small and large, contributing to the progress of the attack and to the development of the overall battle. "Actions along one wing would contribute to those on the other. A defensive action by one corps might enable another to move forward." All commanders would be expected to constantly disrupt, spoil, or preempt enemy preparations.

26. This is the first mention we can find of the use of "operation" with its special meaning. See Baron Colmar Von der Goltz, "The Operations" Section 8, *The Conduct of War*, 1895. A photocopy of this document, produced by the U.S. Army War College Art of War Colloquium in February 1983, is in the possession of the authors. It is noteworthy that this definition appeared in the U.S. Army publication, "The Principles of Strategy" (1920), which was intended to provide an American text for the General Staff School to replace Von der Goltz' original. On this basis, the idea of "Operations" as a cluster of tactical actions connected by a unifying idea was already established in U.S. understanding prior to 1920 but had somehow been lost until it was resurrected by in FM 100-5 in 1982. See Michael Matheny, *In the Beginning*, unreferenced photocopy passed to the authors by Colonel Matheny in 2001.

27. Prussian Field Service Regulations 1869; Michael D. Krause, "Moltke and the Origins of the Operational Level of War," *Military Review*, September 1990.

28. *Moltke on the Art of War*, pp. 13, 36.

29. Hughes, p. 47.

30. *Ibid.*, p. 45.

31. Carl von Clausewitz, Hans Gatzke, ed., *Principles of War*, Harrisburg, PA: The Military Service Publishing Company, 1948, p. 46.

32. By way of contrast, in much of our practice today we have stepped away from strategies of annihilation to embrace strategies of exhaustion. In this, annihilation is focused on the destruction of the military capacity of the enemy in order to be able to dictate the terms of the peace, and exhaustion is focused on denying a more powerful enemy victory long enough to exhaust him physically, morally, or politically. Admittedly, these are in practice two extremes on a continuum, with both being in play in most wars, but it is important for our purposes to isolate them in terms of their intent. Annihilation is the customary western approach to war. Of course, wars do not end until one of the belligerents accepts that he is beaten. Annihilation attempts to crush the enemy's **will** to resist by destroying his **ability** to resist, allowing the victor

to dictate subsequent events. A strategy of exhaustion, on the other hand, tries to get to Clausewitz' third point more directly, by convincing the enemy that victory is either unachievable or, if achievable, that the fruits of victory are not worth the trouble being taken. Exhaustion is the classic strategy of the insurgent.

33. Clausewitz, p. 91.

34. Walter Goerlitz, *The German General Staff*, New York: Praeger, 1953, p. 92.

35. Echavarria, p. 211, establishes that these understandings had taken root in Germany as well as in imperial Russia.

36. John Keegan, *Mask of Command*, London, UK: Pimlico, 2004, p. 248.

37. Arden Bucholz, *Moltke, Schlieffen and Prussian War Planning*, Oxford, UK: Berg Publishers, 1991, p. 314.

38. *Ibid.*, p. 2.

39. *Ibid.*, p. 147.

40. Dieter Brand, "The Origins of Freie Operationen," *Military Review*, July/August 2000, discusses the concept in some detail.

41. Barbara Tuchman, "Von Kluck's Turn," Chapter 21, *The Guns of August*, New York: Macmillan Publishing Company, 1988, discusses this decision and its consequences in some detail.

42. Matthew Cooper, *The German Army 1933-45: Its Political and Military Failure*, London, UK: Macdonald and Janes, 1978, p. 133.

43. *Ibid.*, p. 134.

44. Erich von Manstein, *Lost Victories*, London, UK: Greenhill Books, Herts, 1987, is the best reference for the development of Fall. Robert A. Doughty, *The Breaking Point: Sedan and the Fall of France*, Hamden, CT: Archon, 1990, is best for a description of Guderian's operations. Guderian is interesting because, taking

freie operationen to the extreme, he was largely responsible for dragging his superiors across France while they resisted his progress as best they could.

45. Manstein, pp. 175-178.

46. Much of the detail for this section is taken from U.S. Department of the Army, *The German Campaign in Russia: Planning and Operations (1940-42)*, Washington, DC, 1955, pp. 6-36.

47. The placement of officers of the General Staff as Chiefs of Staff and operations officers at each Headquarters down to at least Corps level and sometimes lower made German operational planning more collaborative and less hierarchical than our understanding of the Anglophone equivalents. With each of these officers bringing the particular focus of his formation but the shared perspective of the General Staff, this, in turn, supported the maintenance of intimacy in the conversation between strategy and tactics.

48. Alan Clark, *Barbarossa*, London, UK: Cassell, 2005, p. 144.

49. Matthew Cooper, *The German Army 1939-1945*, p. 290. There is not space here to discuss German operational art during defensive maneuver but there are good examples in both Russia and France of that aspect.

50. Orenstein, pp. xiii-xviii, describes this taxonomy in detail.

51. A. A. Svechin, *Strategy and Operational Art*, in Orenstein, p. 7.

52. I. Mariyevsky, *Formation and Development of the Theory of Operational art (1918-38)*, in Orenstein, p. 306.

53. James. J. Schneider, *The Structure of a Strategic Revolution*, Novato CA: Presidio Press, 1994, traces the entire debate in some detail.

54. Mariyevsky, p. 307, notes that, at least initially based on the lessons of World War I, Frunze held the contrary position "one could not place before oneself the aim of 'destroying' the

enemy. . . . This is a dream that cannot be fulfilled." Svechin put forward similar views in *Strategy and Operational Art*, pp. 9-13.

55. Schneider, p. 177.

56. *Ibid.*, p. 178. (As an aside—the soldierly hubris that "today's wars are different from yesterday's wars" is salient here. Cf. Clausewitz, "As a rule destroying the enemy's forces tends to be a gradual process," p. 90.

57. M. Tukhachevskiy, "Voyna klopov," *Revolyustiya I voyna*, No. 22, 1923, quoted in Jacob Kipp, "Two Views of Warsaw: The Russian Civil War and Soviet Operational Art, 1920-1932," in B. J. McKerchner and M. C. Hennessy, eds., *The Operational Art: Developments in the Theory of War*, Westport, CT: Praeger, 1996, p. 53. Tukhachevskiy wrote the Preface to the Russian version of Fuller's *Reformation of War* in which he takes the time to challenge much of what Fuller had to say. The Foreword in its entirety is reproduced in R. E. Simpkin, *Deep Battle, The Brainchild of Marshal Tukhachevsky*, London, UK: Brassey's Defence Publishers, pp. 125-134.

58. Tukhachevskiy considered encirclement to be the optimum outcome of the deep attack and discusses it in some depth in *New Problems in Warfare*.

59. G. Isserson, "Operational Prospects for the Future," H. S. Orenstein, ed., *The Evolution of Soviet Operational Art: The Documentary Basis*, Portland, OR: Frank Cass, 1995, p. 81.

60. Kipp, p. 309.

61. E. F. Ziemke, "The Soviet Theory of Deep Operations," *Parameters*, Vol. XIII, No. 2, 1982.

62. The most informative account of post-World War II Soviet developments we have found is David M. Glantz, "Soviet Operational Art Since 1936: 'The Triumph of Maneuver War'," in Bruce W. Menning, ed., *Historical Perspectives of the Operational Art*.

63. Svechin, quoted in Schneider, p. 175.

64. Triandafillov, "The Nature of Operations of Modern Armies," quoted in Schneider, p. 191.

65. Svechin, p. 6.

66. J. Kipp, "Two Views of Warsaw: The Russian Civil War and Soviet Operational Art, 1920-1932," in McKerchner and Hennessy, p. 74. By the end of World War II, Soviet thinking had begun to encompass the "salient thrust" which was a deep attack intended not at encirclement but at splitting or shattering the defensive front. This reflected the Soviets' overwhelming and growing materiel superiority over their German enemy and the Hitler-directed propensity for German forces to stay in place. The end result—annihilation—was the same.

67. Isserson, p. 66; and Schneider, p. 185.

68. George Orwell's review of Liddell Hart, "The British Way in Warfare," *New Statesman*, November 21, 1942, quoted in Gat Azar, *A History of Military Thought*, Oxford, CT: Oxford University Press, 2001, p. 685.

69. J. S. Corum, *The Roots of Blitzkrieg*, Lawrence: University of Kansas Press, 1992, analyzes the development of Blitzkrieg, and in pp. 139-141, the role of British theorists, in some detail. Although the Germans were certainly aware of Fuller in particular and Liddell-Hart to a lesser extent, it would be unreasonable to ascribe to either more than a marginal and diffuse influence.

70. For summaries of the debate about the British contribution to the birth of Blitzkrieg, see Azar Gat, "Liddell-Hart's Theory of Armoured Warfare: Revising the Revisionists," *The Journal of Strategic Studies*, Vol. 19, No. 1, March 1996, pp. 1-30; and Brian Holden Reid, *Studies in British Military Thought—Debates with Fuller and Liddell-Hart*, Lincoln: University of Nebraska Press, 1998.

71. This discussion is taken from Reid, pp. 74-75.

72. Tukhachevskiy, p. 53.

73. B. H. Liddell-Hart, *Strategy*, New York: Meridian, 1991, p. 324. For clarity in this monograph, the authors have here substituted operational art for Liddell-Hart's usage of "Strategy."

74. *Ibid.*, p. 326.

75. Gat, "Liddell-Hart: Revising the Revisionists," p. 11.

76. At the time he was writing "Strategy," Liddell-Hart was also working on his excellent study of *Sherman: Soldier, Realist, American*, London, UK: Dodd, Mead and Co., 1929.

77. Gat, "Liddell-Hart: Revising the Revisionists," p. 9.

78. *Ibid.*, p. 14; Liddell-Hart, "Strategy," p. 326. This provides further and important contrast to the Soviet approach to operational art in which they perceived the logistics of sustaining striking power into depth as being as important as the actual fighting. Soviet operational art, being about the application of mass, is logistics-based.

79. Liddell-Hart, "Strategy," p. 327.

80. From an article in *The Times*, September 18, 1935, quoted in Gat, "Liddell-Hart: Revising the Revisionists," p. 11.

81. Naveh.

82. It could be argued that in his discussion of Soviet operational theory, Naveh overplays the role of systems theory. No soldier can fail to have a systems view of warfare — everything is clearly connected with everything else — and for the Soviets, this view, filtered through Marxist reductionism, leads to enormously detailed analysis of the multiple resultant interactions. Although systems thinking was apparent in many sociological, economic, and natural history tracts (Darwin's *Origin of Species*, for example) in the late 19th and early 20th centuries, general systems theory as an independent body of thought did not emerge until the second half of the 20th century and is unlikely to have influenced Tukhachevskiy and his colleagues who, with the exception of Isserson, were by that time dead.

83. Naveh, p. 16. On p. 17 he lists the means of imposing operational shock as isolating the commander from the system, separating the layers of the hierarchy(CINC from JTF, JTF from Corps, Corps from Division) and actions to suppress the enemy system across its front and through its depth.

84. The Tukhachevskiy quote above is worth repeating in this context: "[A]n operation is the organized struggle of each of the armies for the destruction of the men and material of the other. Not the destruction of some hypothetical, abstract nervous system of the army, but destruction of the real organism — the troops and real nervous system of the opponent, the army's communications, must be the operational goal."

85. The Soviet term "shock" as in "shock army" requires some explanation here. Shock armies were combined arms formations intended to break into the enemy defense and develop the penetration through the defensive zone. Once they had secured a breach and established a bridgehead beyond the defensive zone, "mobile forces" (initially overwhelmingly tank-heavy and subsequently a little more balanced in terms of combined arms) would exploit the penetration and develop it to the objectives of the operation. The Operational Maneuver Group, for example, was a "mobile," not a "shock" formation. Naveh is asking us to accept that in Soviet terminology shock troops did not shock but mobile formations did.

86. In *Strategy*, p. 336, for example, Liddell-Hart lists a number of points as "the concentrated essence of strategy" that present a reasonable starting point for any planner: adjust your ends to your means; keep the object always in mind; choose the line (or course) of least expectation; exploit the line of least resistance; take a line of operation which offers alternative objectives; ensure that both plan and dispositions are flexible; do not throw your weight into a stroke where your opponent is on guard; and do not attack along the same line (or in the same form) after it has once failed.

87. The British School's focus on the psychological impact persists today in the ideas underpinning effects-based operations, some of the more extreme aspirations for network-centric warfare, and some approaches to counterinsurgency. The

efficacy, as opposed to the attractiveness, of these ideas remains undemonstrated.

88. Quoted in Eliot Cohen, *Supreme Command: Soldiers, Statesmen and Leadership in Wartime*, New York: Free Press, 2002, p. 51.

89. Donn A. Starry, one of the prime movers behind the doctrine, explains in "A Perspective on American Military Thought," *Military Review*, July 1989, p. 9, that it was intended as a response to growing Soviet conventional strength and effective nuclear parity. Also, although not stated explicitly in the manual, the challenge for American arms that it identifies — "an enemy who expects to sustain rapid maneuver in the offense," the expectation of facing "large numbers of high quality weapon systems; air and ground maneuver forces; conventional, nuclear and chemical fires; unconventional warfare; active reconnaissance, and target acquisition efforts; and electronic warfare" — are a close match to those expected on the NATO battlefield.

90. Emphasis in **design** added. Australia defines the operational level of war as "the planning and conduct of campaigns and major operations in order to achieve strategic objectives" (ADDP-D 2002, para 3-9). British Defence Doctrine (JDPO-01 2008, para 231) describes the operational level of war as "the level at which campaigns are planned, conducted and sustained within a theatre or area of operations."

91. A. F. Lykke, "Toward an Understanding of Military Strategy," *Military Review*, May 1989, p. 3.

92. Cohen, Appendix.

93. Samuel P. Huntington, *The Soldier and the State: The Theory and Politics of Civil-Military Relations*, New York: Vintage Books, 1964, pp. 307-308.

94. *Ibid.*, p. 308; and Cohen, p. 228.

95. Cohen, p. 229. The Weinberger doctrine was formulated by U.S. SECDEF Caspar Weinberger for a speech at the National Press Club in the wake of the 1983 excursion into Lebanon. It

states, *inter alia,* that the United States should not commit forces to combat unless the vital national interests of the US or its allies are involved; that they should only be committed wholeheartedly and with the clear intention of winning; and that they should only be committed with clearly defined political and military objectives. The Powell Doctrine was an expansion of the Weinberger doctrine articulated by the then Chairman of the Joint Chiefs of Staff General Colin Powell. Powell reinforced Weinberger's points above and added that all nonviolent policy measures needed to have been fully exhausted, that a plausible exit strategy needed to have been identified, that the full consequences of U.S. actions needed to have been fully considered, and that the action have the support of U.S. domestic and of the wider international audiences.

96. Antulio Echevarria, *Towards An American Way of War,* Carlisle, PA: Strategic Studies Institute, U.S. Army War College, March 2004, p. v. To support this proposition, he cites Russell Weigley, *The American Way of War: A History of United States Military Strategy and Policy,* Bloomington: Indiana University Press, 1977; and Max Boot, *The Savage Wars of Peace: Small Wars and the Rise of Peace,* New York: Da Capo Press, 2003, p. 16. He argues later that much like its predecessor, the current American way of war focuses principally on defeating the enemy in battle. Its underlying concepts are a polyglot of information-centric theories such as network-centric warfare, rapid decisive operations, and shock and awe that center on "taking down" an opponent quickly, rather than finding ways to apply military force in the pursuit of broader political aims. Moreover, the characteristics of the U.S. style of warfare — speed, jointness, knowledge, and precision — are better suited for strike operations than for translating such operations into strategic successes.

97. An illustration of the close coupling of strategy and tactics occurred in Iraq in 2007. During the Surge, the selected counterinsurgency approach was "Clear-Hold-Build." Buried deep in the "hold" part was a decision to encircle cleared areas of Baghdad with concrete "T-Walls" to prevent reinfiltration by insurgents. This simple and successful tactical measure was discussed and variously criticized in the Iraqi parliament, the U.S. Congress, the UN, the various parliaments that comprise Europe, and the international news media.

98. The discussion of the Falklands War rests heavily on Max Hastings and Simon Jenkins, *The Battle for the Falklands*, London, UK: Michael Joseph, 1983.

99. *Ibid.*, p. 231.

100. We will admit here to sharing the "hubris of the present." Clausewitz, pp. 608-609, notes that:

> If war is to be fully consonant with political objectives, and policy suited to the means available for war, then unless statesman and soldier are combined in one person, the only sound expedient is to make the commander-in-chief a member of the cabinet, so that the cabinet can share in the major aspects of his activities. But that, in turn, is only feasible if the cabinet — that is, the government — is near the theatre of operations, so that decisions can be taken without serious loss of time.

Even in 1982 the state of electronic communications enabled the British cabinet to be "close" enough to the theater of operations to be involved in the major aspects of the campaign commander's activities.

101. Bob Woodward, *The War Within: A Secret White House History*, New York: Simon and Schuster, 2008.

102. For example, a 1955 German definition provided by General Hans Speidel states, "Operations . . . is the conduct of a series of engagements dependent on each other in time, space, and effect, on the battlefield, and in accordance with the tasks presented by strategic planning." J. L. Wallach, *The Dogma of the Battle of Annihilation: The Theories of Clausewitz and Schlieffen and Their Impact on the German Conduct of Two World Wars*, Westport, CT: Greenwood Press, 1986, p. 11.

103. Qiao Liang and Wang Xiangsui, *Unrestricted Warfare*, Beijing, China: People's Liberation Army Literature and Arts Publishing House, February 1999. Other particularly valuable publications are Michael Evans, "From Kadesh to Kandahar: Military Theory and the Future of War," *Naval War College Review*, Summer 2003; Frank Hoffman, *Hybrid Wars*, Arlington,

VA: Potomac Institute for Policy Studies, 2007; Australian Army, *Complex Warfighting*, Army Headquarters, Canberra ACT 2003; and U.S. Joint Forces Command, *Joint Operating Environment: Trends and Challenges for the Future Joint Operating Force through 2030*, Norfolk, VA, 2007.

104. Qiao Liang and Wang Xiangsui, p. 162.

105. *Ibid.*, p. 206.

106. Again, this idea is not entirely novel. Robert Osgood, perhaps America's leading theorist of limited war during the Cold War, maintained that, even in an age laboring under the shadow of nuclear escalation, the use of military force as a rational extension of policy still had a place, providing one measured success "only in political terms and not purely in terms of crushing the enemy." Robert E. Osgood, *Limited War: The Challenge to American Strategy*, Chicago: University of Chicago Press, 1957, p. 22. The idea is also picked up in U.S. Joint Command, p. 64.

> While the adversary will not attempt to hold ground or conduct combined arms warfare against U.S. territory, warfare will be conducted as strikes that focus on the erosion of national will by violent attacks against civilians, and to disrupt our ability to fight abroad by attacking critical nodes in those systems vital to support military operations. Over time, the adversary hopes to cause the withdrawal or disengagement of opposing U.S. forces and capabilities — without having to actually engage and defeat our military forces in the field. All capabilities will be aimed at exhausting the U.S. strategically over time.

107. Qiao Liang and Wang Xiangsui, pp. 206-214.

108. U.S. Joint Forces Command, p. 67.

109. *Ibid.*, p. 65.

110. Australian Army, *Adaptive Campaigning*, Army Headquarters, Canberra ACT, 2009; The Joint Doctrine & Concepts Centre, Joint Doctrine Note 4/05, *The Comprehensive Approach*, Shrivenham, SWINDON Wilts, UK: Ministry of Defence.

111. Shelby Foote, "Another Grand Design," *The Civil War, A Narrative*, Vol. VII, New York: Random House, 1974, p. 8.

112. Mark Grimsley, "Surviving Military Revolution: The U.S. Civil War," in MacGregor Knox and Williamson Murray, eds., *The Dynamics of Military Revolution 1300-2050*, Cambridge, MA: Cambridge University Press, 2001, p. 82.

113. Villacres, p. 11.

114. US Joint Forces Command, p. 67.

115. Clausewitz, *On War*, p. 606.

ABOUT THE AUTHORS

JUSTIN KELLY retired from the Australian Army in 2007 as a Brigadier. An Armor officer, his last postings in Australia were as Director General of Future Land Warfare in Army Headquarters and Commander of the Land Warfare Development Centre. His operational appointments included command of the Peace Monitoring Group on Bougainville, deputy command of the United Nations peacekeeping force in East Timor, and Director of Strategic Operations in Headquarters Multi-National Force-Iraq. Brigadier Kelley is a graduate of the Royal Military College Duntroon, Royal Military College of Science (UK), Army Command and Staff College, Joint Service Staff College, and the U.S. Army War College.

MICHAEL BRENNAN currently holds the appointment of Director of General Simulation in the Australian Department of Defence. His recent appoint-ments include periods as Research Leader Human Systems Integration within Australia's Defence Science and Technology Organisation and Scientific Adviser–Army. He was attached to the USMC Warfighting Laboratory during 1998-1999. Dr. Brennan holds a Ph.D. in Physics from the Flinders University of South Australia.

The authors have collaborated for over a decade on aspects of capability and concept development and in the development of the Australian Army's military experimentation system.

CPSIA information can be obtained at www.ICGtesting.com
Printed in the USA
LVOW130734100812

293631LV00003B/280/P